Certified Cloud Security Professional (CCSP)

Practice Questions

www.ipspecialist.net

[Document Control]

Proposal Name	:	CCSP – Practice Questions
Document Version	:	1
Document Release Date	:	24 May 2019
Reference	:	IPSpecialist_PQ_CCSP

Feedback:

If you have any comments regarding the quality of this book, or otherwise alter it to better suit your needs, you can contact us through email at info@ipspecialist.net

Please make sure to include the book title and ISBN in your message

About IPSpecialist

IPSPECIALIST LTD. IS COMMITTED TO EXCELLENCE AND DEDICATED TO YOUR SUCCESS.

Our philosophy is to treat our customers like family. We want you to succeed, and we are willing to do anything possible to help you make it happen. We have the proof to back up our claims. We strive to accelerate billions of careers with great courses, accessibility, and affordability. We believe that continuous learning and knowledge evolution are most important things to keep re-skilling and up-skilling the world.

Planning and creating a specific goal is where IPSpecialist helps. We can create a career track that suits your visions as well as develop the competencies you need to become a professional Network Engineer. We can also assist you with the execution and evaluation of proficiency level based on the career track you choose, as they are customized to fit your specific goals.

We help you STAND OUT from the crowd through our detailed IP training content packages.

Course Features:

- *Self-Paced learning*
    - O Learn at your own pace and in your own time
- *Covers Complete Exam Blueprint*
    - O Prep-up for the exam with confidence
- *Case Study Based Learning*
    - O Relate the content with real life scenarios
- *Subscriptions that suits you*
    - O Get more pay less with IPS Subscriptions
- *Career Advisory Services*
    - O Let industry experts plan your career journey
- *Virtual Labs to test your skills*
    - O With IPS vRacks, you can testify your exam preparations
- *Practice Questions*
    - O Practice Questions to measure your preparation standards
- *On Request Digital Certification*
    - O On request digital certification from IPSpecialist LTD.

About the Authors:

This book has been compiled with the help of multiple professional engineers. These engineers specialize in different fields e.g Networking, Security, Cloud, Big Data, IoT etc. Each engineer develops content in its specialized field that is compiled to form a comprehensive certification guide.

About the Technical Reviewers:

Nouman Ahmed Khan

AWS-Architect, CCDE, CCIEX5 (R&S, SP, Security, DC, Wireless), CISSP, CISA, CISM is a Solution Architect working with a major telecommunication provider in Qatar. He works with enterprises, mega-projects, and service providers to help them select the best-fit technology solutions. He also works closely as a consultant to understand customer business processes and helps select an appropriate technology strategy to support business goals. He has more than 14 years of experience working in Pakistan/Middle-East & UK. He holds a Bachelor of Engineering Degree from NED University, Pakistan, and M.Sc. in Computer Networks from the UK.

Abubakar Saeed

Abubakar Saeed has more than twenty-five years of experience in Managing, Consulting, Designing, and implementing large-scale technology projects, extensive experience heading ISP operations, solutions integration, heading Product Development, Presales, and Solution Design. Emphasizing on adhering to Project timelines and delivering as per customer expectations, he always leads the project in the right direction with his innovative ideas and excellent management.

Muhammad Yousuf

Muhammad Yousuf is a professional technical content writer. He is Certified Ethical Hacker (CEHv10) and Cisco Certified Network Associate (CCNA) in Routing and Switching. He holds a Bachelor's Degree in Telecommunication, Engineering from Sir Syed University of Engineering and Technology. He has both technical knowledge and industry sounding information, which he uses perfectly in his career.

Farah Qadir

Farah Qadir is a professional technical content writer, holding Bachelor's Degree in Telecommunication Engineering from Sir Syed University of Engineering and Technology. With strong educational background, she possesses exceptional researching and writing skills that has led her to impart knowledge through her professional career.

Muhammad Khawar

Muhammad Khawar is a professional technical content writer. He holds a Bachelor's Degree in Computer Science from Virtual University of Pakistan. He was working as an IT Executive in a reputable organization. He has completed his training of CCNA Routing and Switching, .NET and Web designing. He as both technical knowledge and industry sounding information.

Free Resources:

With each workbook bought from Amazon, IPSpecialist offers free resources to our valuable customers.

Once you buy this book you will have to contact us at support@ipspecialist.net or tweet @ipspecialistnet to get this limited time offer without any extra charges.

Free Resources Include:

Exam Practice Questions in Quiz Simulation: IP Specialists' Practice Questions have been developed keeping in mind the certification exam perspective. The collection of these questions from our technology workbooks is prepared keeping the exam blueprint in mind, covering not only important but necessary topics as well. It is an ideal document to practice and revise your certification.

Career Report: This report is a step by step guide for a novice who wants to develop his/her career in the field of computer networks. It answers the following queries:

- Current scenarios and future prospects.
- Is this industry moving towards saturation or are new opportunities knocking at the door?
- What will the monetary benefits be?
- Why to get certified?
- How to plan and when will I complete the certifications if I start today?
- Is there any career track that I can follow to accomplish specialization level?

Furthermore, this guide provides a comprehensive career path towards being a specialist in the field of networking and also highlights the tracks needed to obtain certification.

IPS Personalized Technical Support for Customers: Good customer service means helping customers efficiently, in a friendly manner. It is essential to be able to handle issues for customers and do your best to ensure they are satisfied. Providing good service is one of the most important things that can set our business apart from the others of its kind.

Great customer service will result in attracting more customers and attain maximum customer retention.

IPS is offering personalized TECH support to its customers to provide better value for money. If you have any queries related to technology and labs you can simply ask our technical team for assistance via Live Chat or Email.

Become an Author & Earn with Us

If you are interested in becoming an author and start earning passive income, IPSpecialist offers "Earn with us" program. We all consume, develop and create content during our learning process, certification exam preparations, and during searching, developing and refining our professional careers. That content, notes, guides, worksheets and flip cards among other material is normally for our own reference without any defined structure or special considerations required for formal publishing.

IPSpecialist can help you craft this 'draft' content into a fine product with the help of our global team of experts. We sell your content via different channels as:

1. Amazon – Kindle
2. eBay
3. LuLu
4. Kobo
5. Google Books
6. Udemy and many 3rd party publishers and resellers

Our Products

Technology Workbooks

IPSpecialist Technology workbooks are the ideal guides to developing the hands-on skills necessary to pass the exam. Our workbook covers official exam blueprint and explains the technology with real life case study based labs. The content covered in each workbook consists of individually focused technology topics presented in an easy-to-follow, goal-oriented, systematic approach. Every scenario features detailed breakdowns and thorough verifications to help you completely understand the task and associated technology.

We extensively used mind maps in our workbooks to visually explain the technology. Our workbooks have become a widely used tool to learn and remember the information effectively.

vRacks

Our highly scalable and innovative virtualized lab platforms let you practice the IP Specialist Technology Workbook at your own time and your own place as per your convenience.

Quick Reference Sheets

Our quick reference sheets are a concise bundling of condensed notes of the complete exam blueprint. It is an ideal and handy document to help you remember the most important technology concepts related to the certification exam.

Practice Questions

IP Specialists' Practice Questions are dedicatedly designed from a certification exam perspective. The collection of these questions from our technology workbooks are prepared keeping the exam blueprint in mind covering not only important but necessary topics as well. It's an ideal document to practice and revise your certification.

Our Products

Technology Workbooks

IPSpecialist Technology workbooks are the ideal guides to developing the hands-on skills necessary to pass the exam. Our workbook covers official exam blueprint and explains the technology with real life case study based labs. The content covered in each workbook consists of individually focused technology topics presented in an easy-to-follow, goal-oriented, step-by-step approach. Every scenario features detailed breakdowns and thorough verifications to help you completely understand the task and associated technology.

We extensively used mind maps in our workbooks to visually explain the technology. Our workbooks have become a widely used tool to learn and remember the information effectively.

vRacks

Our highly scalable and innovative virtualized lab platforms let you practice the IP Specialist Technology Workbook at your own time and your own place as per your convenience.

Quick Reference Sheets

Our quick reference sheets are a concise bundling of condensed notes of the complete exam blueprint for CCSP. It's an ideal handy document to help you remember the most important technology concepts related to CCSP exam.

Practice Questions

IP Specialists' Practice Questions are dedicatedly designed for certification exam perspective. The collection of these questions from our technology workbooks are prepared to keep the exam blueprint in mind covering not only important but necessary topics as well. It's an ideal document to practice and revise your certification.

About the CCSP Exam

CCSP Linear Examination Information

Length of exam:	4 hours
Number of questions:	125
Question format:	Multiple choice
Passing grade:	700 out of 1000 points
Exam language availability:	English
Testing centre:	Pearson VUE

The Certified Cloud Security Professional (CCSP) is the most globally recognized certification in the information security market. CCSP validates an information security professional's deep technical and managerial knowledge and experience to design, manage and secure data, applications and infrastructure in the cloud using best practices, policies and procedure established by the cybersecurity experts at (ISC)2.

The broad spectrum of topics included in the CCSP ensures its relevancy across all disciplines in the field of information security. Successful candidates are competent in the following 6 domains:

1. Architectural Concepts & Design Requirements
2. Cloud Data Security
3. Cloud Platform & Infrastructure Security
4. Cloud Application Security
5. Operations
6. Legal & Compliance

Experience Requirements

Candidates must have a minimum of 5 years cumulative paid full-time work experience in 2 or more of the 6 domains of the CCSP CBK. Earning CSA's CCSK certificate can be substituted for 1 year of experience in 1 or more of the 6 domains of the CCSP CBK. Earning (ISC)²'s CISSP credential can be substituted for the entire CCSP experience requirement.

A candidate that doesn't have the required experience to become a CCSP may become an Associate of (ISC)² by successfully passing the CCSP examination. The Associate of (ISC)² will then have 6 years to earn the 5 years required experience.

Accreditation

CCSP under ANSI review for compliance with the stringent requirements of ANSI/ISO/IEC Standard 17024.

How do CCSP Certifications Help?

The most-esteemed cybersecurity certification in the world. The CCSP recognizes information security leaders who understand cybersecurity strategy, as well as hands-on implementation. It shows you have the knowledge and experience to design, develop and manage the overall security posture of an organization. Are you ready to prove you are an expert?

Ideal for:

Experienced, high-achieving information security professionals

Why Pursue It:

Career Game-Changer: The CCSP can catapult your career, leading to more credibility, better opportunities, higher pay and more.

Ongoing Growth and Learning: You will expand your skills, knowledge, and network of experts so that you can stay at the forefront of your craft.

A Mighty Challenge. You love to push yourself. You will feel complete exhilaration when you pass our rigorous exam and join this elite community.

Experience Required:

Candidates must have a minimum of five years cumulative, paid, full-time work experience in two or more of the six domains of the CCSP Common Body of Knowledge (CBK).

Only a one-year experience exemption is granted for education.

(ISC)² Certifications

Information security careers can feel isolating! When you certify, you become a member of (ISC)² — a leading community of cybersecurity professionals. You can collaborate with thought leaders, network with global peers, expand your skills and so much more. It is a community that's here to support you throughout your career.

Figure 1: ISC² Certifications Track

Practice Questions:

Questions

1. Identify the most common cloud service model in the given options:
   A. Infrastructure as a Service
   B. Software as a Service
   C. Platform as a Service
   D. All of the above
   E. None of the above

2. Identify the technologies that have made cloud service viable in the given options:
   A. Virtualization
   B. Widely available broadband
   C. Cryptographic connectivity
   D. Smart hubs

3. Cloud vendors are held to legal obligations with determined metrics by:
   A. SLAs
   B. Regulations
   C. Law
   D. Discipline

4. What is the main reason behind in the CIA triad, if a cloud customer cannot get access to the cloud services?
   A. Integrity
   B. Authentication
   C. Confidentiality
   D. Availability

5. Identify the service that offers by the Cloud Access Security Brokers (CASB).
   A. Single sign-on
   B. BC/DR/COOP
   C. IAM
   D. Key escrow

6. Identify the media, which cannot be encrypted.
   A. Storage
   B. Remote access
   C. Secure sessions
   D. Magnetic swipe cards

7. Identify the main reason an organization wants to migrate to cloud.
   A. Low costs
   B. Elimination of risks
   C. Reduced operational expenses
   D. Increased efficiency

8. Identify the term, which is not related to cloud computing.
   A. On-demand services
   B. Negating the need for backups
   C. Resource pooling
   D. Measured or metered service

9. Identify the term that can result in vendor lock-in.
   A. Unfavorable contract
   B. Statutory compliance
   C. Proprietary data formats
   D. Insufficient bandwidth

10. _____ happens when a cloud customer cannot recover or access their own data.
    A. Vendor closure
    B. Vendor lock-out
    C. Vendor lock-in
    D. Vending route

11. Identify the features of cloud computing.
    A. Broad network access
    B. Reversed charging configuration
    C. Rapid scaling
    D. On-demand self-service

12. Who is responsible for the security of PII, when a cloud customer uploads PII to a cloud provider?
    A. Cloud provider
    B. Regulators
    C. Cloud customer
    D. The individuals who are the subjects of the PII

13. Which of the following terms signifies the critical paths, processes, and assets of an organization?
    A. Business Requirements

B. BIA

C. RMF

D. CIA Triad

14. Organizational ownership of the infrastructure and the hardware, and usage only by members of that organization: this feature belongs to which of the cloud deployment models?

A. Private

B. Public

C. Hybrid

D. Motive

15. Which cloud deployment model features ownership by a cloud provider, with services that offer multiple resources such as Virtual Machines (VMs), applications or storage and is available to anyone over the internet?

A. Private

B. Public

C. Hybrid

D. Motive

16. Which cloud deployment model provides joint ownership of assets between an affinity group?

A. Private

B. Public

C. Hybrid

D. Community

17. Which cloud service model is best to use if a cloud customer wants to conduct a software for development and testing?

A. IaaS

B. PaaS

C. SaaS

D. Hybrid

18. Which cloud service model is suitable if a cloud customer wants a fully operational environment with little maintenance or administration task?

A. IaaS

B. PaaS

C. SaaS

D. Hybrid

19. Which cloud service model is probably best to use if a cloud customer wants a core environment in which their own organization for BC/DR purposes?
    A. IaaS
    B. PaaS
    C. SaaS
    D. Hybrid

20. Which of the following are components of cloud computing?
    A. Minimal management effort and shared resources
    B. High cost and unique resources
    C. Rapid provisioning and slow release of resources
    D. Limited access and service provider interaction

21. Which one of the followings is a distinguishing characteristic of a managed service provider?
    A. Have some form of a NOC but no help desk.
    B. Be able to monitor and manage objects for the customer remotely and reactively maintain these objects under management.
    C. Have some form of a help desk but no NOC.
    D. Be able to monitor and manage objects for the customer remotely and proactively maintain these objects under management.

22. Identify the cloud computing roles in the given options:
    A. Cloud customer and financial auditor
    B. CSP and backup service provider
    C. Cloud service broker and user
    D. Cloud service auditor and object

23. Identify the essential characteristics of cloud computing in the given options:
    A. On-demand self-service
    B. Unmeasured service
    C. Resource isolation
    D. Broad network access

24. Identify the main building blocks of cloud computing.
    A. Data, access control, virtualization, and services
    B. Storage, networking, printing, and virtualization
    C. CPU, RAM, storage, and networking
    D. Data, CPU, RAM, and access control

25. What is the capability provided to the cloud customer while using an IaaS solution?
    A. To provision processing, storage, networks, and other fundamental computing resources when the consumer is not able to deploy and run arbitrary software, which can include OSs and applications.
    B. To provision processing, storage, networks, and other fundamental computing resources when the provider can deploy and run arbitrary software, which can include OSs and applications.
    C. To provision processing, storage, networks, and other fundamental computing resources when the auditor can deploy and run arbitrary software, which can include OSs and applications.
    D. To provision processing, storage, networks, and other fundamental computing resources when the consumer can deploy and run arbitrary software, which can include OSs and applications.

26. What is the capability provided to the cloud customer while using an IaaS solution?
    A. Metered and priced by units consumed
    B. The ability to scale up infrastructure services based on projected usage
    C. Increased energy and cooling system efficiencies
    D. Transferred cost of ownership

27. What is the key benefit provided to the cloud customer, while using a PaaS solution?
    A. To deploy onto the cloud infrastructure provider-created or acquired applications created using programming languages, libraries, services, and tools that the provider supports. The consumer does not manage or control the underlying cloud infrastructure, including network, servers, operating systems, or storage, but has to control over the deployed applications and possibly configuration settings for the application-hosting environment.
    B. To deploy onto the cloud infrastructure consumer-created or acquired applications created using programming languages, libraries, services, and tools that the provider supports. The provider does not manage or control the underlying cloud infrastructure, including network, servers, operating systems, or storage, but has to control over the deployed applications and possibly configuration settings for the application-hosting environment.
    C. To deploy onto the cloud infrastructure consumer-created or acquired applications created using programming languages, libraries, services, and tools that the provider supports. The consumer does not manage or control the underlying cloud infrastructure, including network, servers, operating systems, or storage, but has to control over the deployed applications and possibly configuration settings for the application-hosting environment.
    D. To deploy onto the cloud infrastructure consumer-created or acquired applications created using programming languages, libraries, services, and tools that the consumer supports. The consumer does not manage or control the

underlying cloud infrastructure, including network, servers, operating systems, or storage, but has to control over the deployed applications and possibly configuration settings for the application-hosting environment.

28. What is the main characteristics or advantages of PaaS?
   A. Support for a homogenous hosting environment
   B. Ability to reduce lock-in
   C. Support for a single programming language
   D. Ability to manually scale

29. What are the critical benefits provided to the customer while using a SaaS solution?
   A. To use the provider's applications running on a cloud infrastructure. The applications are accessible from various client devices through either a thin client interface, such as a web browser (for example, web-based E-mail), or a program interface. The consumer does not manage or control the underlying cloud infrastructure, including network, servers, operating systems, storage, or even individual application capabilities, with the possible exception of limited user-specific application configuration settings.
   B. To use the provider's applications running on a cloud infrastructure. The applications are accessible from various client devices through either a thin client interface, such as a web browser (for example, web-based E-mail), or a program interface. The consumer does manage or control the underlying cloud infrastructure, including network, servers, operating systems, storage, or even individual application capabilities, with the possible exception of limited user-specific application configuration settings.
   C. To use the consumer's applications running on a cloud infrastructure. The applications are accessible from various client devices through either a thin client interface, such as a web browser (for example, web-based E-mail), or a program interface. The consumer does not manage or control the underlying cloud infrastructure including network, servers, operating systems, storage, or even individual application capabilities, with the possible exception of limited user-specific application configuration settings.
   D. To use the consumer's applications running on a cloud infrastructure. The applications are accessible from various client devices through either a thin client interface, such as a web browser (for example, web-based E-mail), or a program interface. The consumer does manage or control the underlying cloud infrastructure, including network, servers, operating systems, storage, or even individual application capabilities, with the possible exception of limited user-specific application configuration settings.

30. Identify the correct cloud-computing model in the given options:

    A. Public, internal, hybrid, and community
    B. External, private, hybrid, and community
    C. Public, private, joint, and community
    D. Public, private, hybrid, and community

31. Identify the main stages of the cloud secure data lifecycle in the given options:
    A. Create, use, store, share, archive, and destroy
    B. Create, store, use, share, archive, and destroy
    C. Create, share, store, archive, use, and destroy
    D. Create, archive, use, share, store, and destroy

32. What are SOC 1, SOC 2, and SOC 3?
    A. Risk management frameworks
    B. Access controls
    C. Audit reports
    D. Software development phases

33. Identify the main Trust Services principles in the given options:
    A. Security, Availability, Processing Integrity, Confidentiality, and Privacy
    B. Security, Auditability, Processing Integrity, Confidentiality, and Privacy
    C. Security, Availability, Customer Integrity, Confidentiality, and Privacy
    D. Security, Availability, Processing Integrity, Confidentiality, and Nonrepudiation

34. For a PaaS solution, identify the main security-related concern in the given options:
    A. Virtual machine attacks
    B. Web application security
    C. Data access and policies
    D. System and resource isolation

35. Gathering business requirements can support the organization in determining all of this information about organizational assets; which of the following is not suitable in this regard?
    A. Full inventory
    B. Usefulness
    C. Value
    D. Criticality

36. The BIA can be used to provide information to which of the following options:
    A. Risk Analysis
    B. Secure Acquisition
    C. BC/DR Planning

   D. Selection of Security Controls

37. To maintain the OS, a customer requires which of the following cloud service models?
   A. CaaS
   B. SaaS
   C. PaaS
   D. IaaS

38. To maintain and update the applications, a customer requires which of the following cloud service models?
   A. CaaS
   B. SaaS
   C. PaaS
   D. IaaS

39. In the SaaS service model, who is responsible for the data?
   A. Customer
   B. Partner
   C. Vendor
   D. None of the above

40. Which of the following options is suitable for the agreement, when the cloud customer and provider negotiate their respective responsibilities and rights about the capabilities and data of the cloud service?
   A. RMF
   B. Contract
   C. MOU
   D. BIA

41. Which type of security control has to include attempting a layered defense?
   A. Technological
   B. Physical
   C. Administrative
   D. All of the above

42. Which one of the followings is not considered an administrative control?
   A. Access control process
   B. Keystroke logging
   C. Door locks
   D. Biometric authentication

43. Which one of the followings is not considered a technological control?
    A. Firewall Software
    B. Fireproof Safe
    C. Fire Extinguisher
    D. Firing Personnel

44. Identify in the given option that is considered a physical control?
    A. Carpets
    B. Ceilings
    C. Doors
    D. Fences

45. Encryption should be used for all of the followings in a cloud environment, except for:
    A. Long-term storage of data
    B. Near-term storage of virtualized images
    C. Secure sessions/VPN
    D. Profile formatting

46. Identify the steps that are involved in the process of hardening a device.
    A. Improve default accounts
    B. Close unused ports
    C. Delete unnecessary services
    D. Strictly control administrator access

47. Which of the following options is not included in the process of hardening a device?
    A. Encrypting the OS
    B. Updating and patching the system
    C. Using video cameras
    D. Performing thorough personnel background checks

48. To create the possibility of processing encrypted data without having to decrypt it, which experimental technology is used in this regard?
    A. Homomorphic
    B. Poly-instantiation
    C. Quantum-state
    D. Gastronomic

49. Which of the following options is determined, if an organization is risk appetite?
    A. Appetite evaluation
    B. Senior management
    C. Legislative mandates

    D. Contractual agreement

50. To reduce risk by applying countermeasures and controls, the remaining, leftover risk is known as:
    A. Null
    B. High
    C. Residual
    D. Pertinent

51. Identify the following options for addressing a risk.
    A. Acceptance
    B. Reversal
    C. Mitigation
    D. Transfer

52. In a BYOD environment to protect data on user devices, the organization has to consider requiring all of the following options; identify it.
    A. DLP Agents
    B. Local Encryption
    C. Multifactor Authentication
    D. Two-person Integrity

53. Which of the following options are means of hardening devices when devices in the cloud datacenter should be secured against attack?
    A. Using a strong password policy
    B. Removing default passwords
    C. Strictly limiting physical access
    D. Removing all admin accounts

54. Identify the following best described risks.
    A. Preventable
    B. Everlasting
    C. The likelihood that a threat will exploit a vulnerability
    D. Transient

55. Before deploying data protection in a cloud environment, what are the three things that you need to understand?
    A. Management, provisioning, and location

    B. Function, location, and actors

    C. Actors, policies, and procedures

    D. Lifecycle, function, and cost

56. Identify the storage types that are used with an Infrastructure as a Service (IaaS) solution.
    A. Volume and Block
    B. Structured and Object
    C. Unstructured and Ephemeral
    D. Volume and Object

57. Identify the storage types that are used with a Platform as a Service (PaaS) solution.
    A. Raw and Block
    B. Structured and Unstructured
    C. Unstructured and Ephemeral
    D. Tabular and Object

58. Identify the options that can be deployed to assist in ensuring the confidentiality of the data in the cloud.

    A. Encryption

    B. Service level agreements

    C. Masking

    D. Continuous monitoring

59. To use a network-based DLP system, where is the place monitoring engine needs to be in order to be deployed?

    A. On a user's workstation

    B. In the storage system

    C. Near the organizational gateway

    D. On a VLAN

60. Where does the encryption engine reside, while using transparent encryption of a database?

    A. At the application using the database

    B. On the instance(s) attached to the volume

    C. In a key management system

D. Within the database

61. Identify the main analysis methods to use with data discovery techniques.
    A. Metadata, labels, and content analysis
    B. Metadata, structural analysis, and labels
    C. Statistical analysis, labels, and content analysis
    D. Bit splitting, labels, and content analysis

62. What is a controller in the context of privacy and data protection?
    A. One who cannot be identified, directly or indirectly, in particular by reference to an identification number or one or more factors specific to his/her physical, physiological, mental, economic, cultural, or social identity.
    B. One who can be identified, directly or indirectly, in particular by reference to an identification number or one or more factors specific to his/her physical, physiological, mental, economic, cultural, or social identity.
    C. The natural or legal person, public authority, agency, or any other body that alone or jointly with others determines the purposes and means of personal processing data.
    D. A natural or legal person, public authority, agency, or any other body that processes personal data on behalf of the customer.

63. Identify which option is related to the Cloud Security Alliance Cloud Controls matrix.
    A. A set of regulatory requirements for cloud service providers
    B. An inventory of cloud service security controls that are arranged into separate security domains
    C. A set of software development lifecycle requirements for cloud service providers
    D. An inventory of cloud service security controls that are arranged into a hierarchy of security domains

64. Identify the standard capabilities of information rights management solutions.
    A. Persistent protection, dynamic policy control, automatic expiration, continuous audit trail, and support for existing authentication infrastructure

B. Persistent protection, static policy control, automatic expiration, continuous audit trail, and support for existing authentication infrastructure

C. Persistent protection, dynamic policy control, manual expiration, continuous audit trail, and support for existing authentication infrastructure

D. Persistent protection, dynamic policy control, automatic expiration, intermittent audit trail, and support for existing authentication infrastructure

65. What are the main components that a data retention policy has to define?

A. Retention periods, data access methods, data security, and data retrieval procedures

B. Retention periods, data formats, data security, and data destruction procedures

C. Retention periods, data formats, data security, and data communication procedures

D. Retention periods, data formats, data security, and data retrieval procedures

66. Identify the methods for the safe disposal of electronic records can always be utilized in a cloud environment.

A. Physical destruction

B. Encryption

C. Overwriting

D. Degaussing

67. Which of the following principles have to be adopted as part of the security operations policies to support continuous operations?

A. Application logging, contract/authority maintenance, secure disposal, and business continuity preparation

B. Audit logging, contract/authority maintenance, secure usage, and incident response legal preparation

C. Audit logging, contract/authority maintenance, secure disposal, and incident response legal preparation

D. Transaction logging, contract/authority maintenance, secure disposal, and disaster recovery preparation

68. Which of the followings is a method of data discovery?
    A. Content-based
    B. User-based
    C. Label-based
    D. Metadata-based

69. Which of the followings is included in the Data labels?
    A. Date data was created
    B. Data owner
    C. Data value
    D. Data for scheduled destruction

70. Which of the followings are data analytics modes?
    A. Real-time analytics
    B. Datamining
    C. Agile business intelligence
    D. Refractory iterations

71. Which of the followings is included in the data labels?
    A. Source
    B. Delivery vendor
    C. Handling restrictions
    D. Jurisdiction

72. Who is the data owner in the cloud motif?
    A. In another jurisdiction
    B. The cloud customer
    C. The cloud provider
    D. The cloud access security broker

73. Which of the following options could be included in the Data labels?
    A. Confidentiality level
    B. Distribution limitations
    C. Access restrictions
    D. Multifactor authentication

74. Who is the data processor usually in the cloud motif?
    A. The party that assigns access rights
    B. The cloud customer
    C. The cloud provider
    D. The cloud access security broker

75. Which of the following options is to related to the security program and process?
    A. Foundational policy
    B. Severe penalties
    C. Multifactor authentication
    D. Homomorphic encryption

76. Which of the following options should the organization include in the policies?
    A. Policy Maintenance
    B. Policy Review
    C. Policy Enforcement
    D. Policy Adjudication

77. Which of the following options is the most pragmatic for data disposal in the cloud?
    A. Melting
    B. Crypto Shredding
    C. Cold Fusion
    D. Overwriting

78. Which option is suitable for intellectual property protection for the tangible expression of a creative idea?
    A. Copyright
    B. Patent
    C. Trademark
    D. Trade secret

79. For a useful manufacturing innovation, what is intellectual property protection?
    A. Copyright
    B. Patent
    C. Trademark
    D. Trade secret

80. Identify the option that is related to intellectual property protection for a precious set of sales leads.
    A. Copyright
    B. Patent
    C. Trademark
    D. Trade secret

81. Which option is suitable for the intellectual property protection for a secret recipe for muffins?
    A. Copyright
    B. Patent
    C. Trademark
    D. Trade secret

82. For the logo of a new video game, what is intellectual property protection?
    A. Copyright
    B. Patent
    C. Trademark

D. Trade secret

83. What aspect is related to the DMCA that has been typically abused and has placed the burden of proof on the accused?

A. Online service provider exemption

B. Decryption program prohibition

C. Takedown notice

D. Puppet plasticity

84. Which federal agency accepts the applications for new patents?

A. USDA

B. USPTO

C. OSHA

D. SEC

85. DRM tools use a multiple forms of methods for enforcement of intellectual property rights. Identify the following options that can be included.

A. Support-based licensing

B. Local agent enforcement

C. Dip switch validity

D. Media-present checks

86. Which of the following regions have at least one country with an overarching, federal privacy law protecting personal data of its citizens?

A. Asia

B. Europe

C. South America

D. The United States

87. Which functions should include DRM solutions?

A. Persistency

B. Automatic Self-destruct

C. Automatic Expiration

D. Dynamic Policy Control

88. Which statement is related to the cloud carrier?

   A. A person, organization, or entity responsible for making a service available to service consumers

   B. The intermediary that provides connectivity and transport of cloud services between CSPs and cloud consumers

   C. A person or organization that maintains a business relationship with, and uses service from, CSPs

   D. The intermediary that provides business continuity of cloud services between cloud service consumers

89. Identify the correct statement regarding SDN.

   A. SDN enables you to execute the control plane software on general-purpose hardware, allowing for the decoupling from specific network hardware configurations and allowing for the use of commodity servers. Further, the use of software-based controllers permits a view of the network that presents a logical switch to the applications running above, allowing for access via APIs that can be used to configure, manage, and secure network resources.

   B. SDN's objective is to provide a clearly defined network control plane to manage network traffic that is not separated from the forwarding plane. This approach allows for network control to become directly programmable and for dynamic adjustment of traffic flows to address changing patterns of consumption.

   C. SDN enables you to execute the control plane software on specific hardware, allowing for the binding of specific network hardware configurations. Further, the use of software-based controllers permits a view of the network that presents a logical switch to the applications running above, allowing for access via APIs that can be used to configure, manage, and secure network resources.

   D. SDN's objective is to offer a clearly defined and separate network control plane to manage network traffic that is separated from the forwarding plane. This approach permits network control to become directly programmable and distinct

from forwarding, allowing for dynamic adjustment of traffic flows to address changing patterns of consumption.

90. What benefits does a reservation provide regarding management of the computing resources of a host in a cloud environment?

A. The ability to arbitrate the issues associated with compute resource contention situations. Resource contention implies that there are too many requests for resources based on the actual available resources currently in the system.

B. A guaranteed minimum resource allocation that must be met by the host with physical compute resources to allow a guest to power on and operate.

C. A maximum ceiling for resource allocation. This ceiling may be fixed, or it may be expandable, allowing for the acquisition of more compute resources through a borrowing scheme from the root resource provider (the host).

D. A guaranteed maximum resource allocation that must be met by the host with physical compute resources to allow a guest to power on and operate.

91. What is the main problem associated with the object storage type that the CCSP should understand?

A. Data consistency, which is achieved only after change propagation to all replica instances has taken place

B. Access control

C. Data consistency, which is achieved only after change propagation to a specified percentage of replica instances has taken place

D. Continuous monitoring

92. Which form of risks are typically related to virtualization?

A. Loss of governance, snapshot and image security, and sprawl

B. Guest breakout, snapshot and image availability, and compliance

C. Guest breakout, snapshot and image security, and sprawl

D. Guest breakout, knowledge level required to manage, and sprawl

93. Who is responsible for application security while using a SaaS solution?

    A. Both the cloud consumer and the enterprise

    B. The enterprise only

    C. The CSP only

    D. The CSP and the enterprise

94. Identify examples of trust zones.

    A. A specific application being used to carry out a general function such as printing

    B. Segmentation according to the department

    C. A web application with a two-tiered architecture

    D. Storage of a baseline configuration on a workstation

95. Identify the relevant cloud infrastructure characteristics that can be considered as distinct advantages in realizing a BCDR plan purpose regarding a cloud-computing environment.

    A. Rapid elasticity, provider-specific network connectivity, and a pay-per-use model

    B. Rapid elasticity, broad network connectivity, and a multitenancy model

    C. Rapid elasticity, broad network connectivity, and a pay-per-use model

    D. Continuous monitoring, broad network connectivity, and a pay-per-use model

96. Which of the following terms are used to describe the practice of obscuring original raw data so that only a portion is displayed for operational purposes?

    A. Tokenization

    B. Data discovery

    C. Obfuscation

    D. Masking

97. Which of the following options can include in the implementation of SIEM solution goals?

    A. Centralization of Log Streams

    B. Trend Analysis

C. Dashboarding

D. Performance Enhancement

98. Which of the following options can be included in the implementation of DLP solution goals?

A. Policy Enforcement

B. Elasticity

C. Data Discovery

D. Loss of Mitigation

99. Which of the followings, due to the loss of deterring, can aid in the DLP solutions?

A. Randomization

B. Inadvertent Disclosure

C. Natural Disaster

D. Device Failure

100. Which experimental technology might lead to the possibility of processing encrypted data without containing to decrypt it initially?

A. AES

B. Link Encryption

C. Homomorphic Encryption

D. One-Time Pads

101. Which of the following functions is required for proper implementation of DLP solution successfully?

A. Accurate Data Categorization

B. Physical Access Limitations

C. USB Connectivity

D. Physical Presence

102. How many databases require implementing tokenization?

A. Two

B. Three

C. Four

D. Five

103. Which of the following functionalities provided can be used by the Data Masking?

A. Secure remote access

B. Enforcing the least privilege

C. Test data in sandboxed environments

D. Authentication of privileged users

104. Which security technology is used to enhance data controls to combine with the DLP?

A. DRM

B. SIEM

C. Kerberos

D. Hypervisors

105. Which department controls the technology exports known as EAR?

A. U.S. State Department

B. U.S. Commerce Department

C. Both of these

D. None of the above

106. Which Department controls the technology exports known as ITAR?

A. U.S. State Department

B. U.S. Commerce Department

C. Both of these

D. None of the above

107. Cryptographic keys for encrypted data stored in the cloud should be _____.
    A. At least 128 bits long
    B. Not stored with the cloud provider
    C. Split into groups
    D. Generated with redundancy

108. Which of the followings can include the best practices for key management?
    A. Have key recovery processes
    B. Maintain key security
    C. Passkeys out of band
    D. Ensure multifactor authentication

109. Why is the cryptographic key secured? Identify the best option.
    A. To a level at least as high as the data, they can decrypt
    B. In vaults
    C. By armed guards
    D. With two-person integrity

110. Which of the followings have to consider when creating plans and policies for data archiving?
    A. Archive Location
    B. The Backup Process
    C. The Format of the Data
    D. The Immediacy of the Technology

111. Identify the correct phases of the data life cycle.
    A. Create, Store, Use, Archive, Share, Destroy
    B. Create, Store, Use, Share, Archive, Destroy
    C. Create, Use, Store, Share, Archive, Destroy
    D. Create, Archive, Store, Share, Use, Destroy

112. Who are third-party providers of IAM functions in the cloud-computing environment?

A. DLPs

B. CASBs

C. SIEMs

D. AESs

113. Which is a cloud storage architecture that handles the data in a hierarchy of files?

A. Object-based Storage

B. File-based Storage

C. Database

D. CDN

114. Which one is a cloud storage architecture that handles the data in caches of copied content close to locations of high demand?

A. Object-based Storage

B. File-based Storage

C. Database

D. CDN

115. Which statement is related to the REST?

A. A protocol specification for exchanging structured information in the implementation of web services in computer networks

B. A software architecture style consisting of guidelines and best practices for creating scalable web services

C. The name of the process that an organization or a person who moves data between CSPs uses to document what he is doing

D. The intermediary process that provides business continuity of cloud services between cloud consumers and CSPs

116. Identify the phases of Software Development Life Cycle model.

A. Planning and requirements analysis, defining, designing, developing, and testing

B. Defining, planning and requirements analysis, designing, developing, and testing

C. Planning and requirements analysis, defining, designing, testing, and developing

D. Planning and requirements analysis, designing, defining, developing, and testing

117. How does the security analyst identify that an attack is an XSS attack?

A. Whenever an application takes trusted data and sends it to a web browser without proper validation or escaping

B. Whenever an application takes untrusted data and sends it to a web browser without proper validation or escaping

C. Whenever an application takes trusted data and sends it to a web browser with proper validation or escaping

D. Whenever an application takes untrusted data and sends it to a web browser with proper validation or escaping

118. Who is a relying party and what does it do in a federated environment?

A. The relying party is the identity provider; it consumes the tokens that the service provider generates.

B. The relying party is the service provider; it consumes the tokens that the customer generates.

C. The relying party is the service provider; it consumes the tokens that the identity provider generates.

D. The relying party is the customer; he consumes the tokens that the identity provider generates.

119. Identify the steps that are used to create an ASMP.

A. Specifying the application requirements and the environment, creating and maintaining the ANF, assessing application security risks, provisioning and operating the application, and auditing the security of the application

B. Assessing application security risks, specifying the application requirements and environment, creating and maintaining the ANF, provisioning and operating the application, and auditing the security of the application

C. Specifying the application requirements and environment, assessing application security risks, provisioning and operating the application, auditing the security of the application, and creating and maintaining the ANF

D. Specifying the application requirements and environment, assessing application security risks, creating and maintaining the ANF, provisioning and operating the application, and auditing the security of the application

120. Which term describes the general ease and efficiency of moving data from one cloud provider to another cloud provider or down from the cloud?

A. Mobility

B. Elasticity

C. Obfuscation

D. Portability

121. Which of the following models are available for cloud BC/DR activities?

A. Private architecture, cloud backup

B. Cloud provider, backup from the same provider

C. Cloud provider, backup from another cloud provider

D. Cloud provider, backup from a private provider

122. Which of the followings are countermeasures for protecting cloud operations against external attackers?

A. Continual monitoring for anomalous activity

B. Detailed and extensive background checks

C. Hardened devices and systems, including servers, hosts, hypervisors, and virtual machines

D. Regular and detailed configuration/change management activities

123. Which of the followings are techniques to improve the portability of cloud data, to reduce the potential of vendor lock-in?

A. Avoid proprietary data formats

B. Use DRM and DLP solutions widely throughout the cloud operation

C. Ensure that there are no physical limitations to moving

D. Ensure favorable contract terms to support portability

124. Identify the techniques that are not used to attenuate risks to the cloud environment, resulting in loss or theft of a device used for remote access.

A. Remote Kill switch

B. Dual Control

C. Muddling

D. Safe Harbor

125. Which of the following are dependencies that must be considered when reviewing the BIA after cloud migration?

A. The cloud provider's suppliers

B. The cloud provider's vendors

C. The cloud provider's utilities

D. The cloud provider's resellers

126. When evaluating the BIA after a cloud migration, the organization have considered new factors related to data breach impacts. One of these new factors is:

A. Legal liability cannot be transferred to the cloud provider

B. Many states have data breach notification laws

C. Breaches can cause a loss of proprietary data

D. Breaches can cause a loss of intellectual property

127. Which cloud computing arrangement entails the cloud customer will have the most control of their data and systems, and the cloud provider will have the least amount of responsibility?

A. IaaS

B. PaaS

C. SaaS

D. Community Cloud

128. After a cloud migration, the BIA has to be updated to include a review of the new risks and impacts linked with cloud operations; this review has to include an analysis of the possibility of vendor lock-in or lock-out. Analysis of this risk may not have to be performed as a new effort, because a lot of the material that would be included is already available from which of the followings?

A. NIST

B. The cloud provider

C. The cost-benefit analysis to the organization conducted when deciding on cloud migration

D. Open source providers

129. A poorly negotiated cloud service contract could result in which of the following detrimental effects?

A. Vendor lock-in

B. Malware

C. Unfavorable terms

D. Lack of necessary services

130. Which of the following risks in the public cloud does not exist in the other cloud service models because of multitenancy?

A. Risk of loss/disclosure due to legal seizures

B. Information bleed

C. DoS/DDoS

D. Escalation of privilege

131. Which of the following countermeasures are taken for protecting cloud operations against internal threats?

A. Aggressive background checks

B. Hardened perimeter devices

C. Skills and knowledge testing

D. Extensive and comprehensive training programs, including initial, recurring, and refresher sessions

132. Which of the following countermeasures are taken for protecting cloud operations against internal threats?

    A. Active physical surveillance and monitoring

    B. Active electronic surveillance and monitoring

    C. Redundant ISPs

    D. Masking and obfuscation of data for all personnel without the need to know for raw data

133. Which of the following countermeasures is taken for protecting cloud operations against internal threats?

    A. Separation of duties

    B. Least privilege

    C. Conflict of interest

    D. Mandatory vacation

134. Which of the followings are benefits for addressing BC/DR offered by cloud operations?

    A. Metered service

    B. Distributed, remote processing, and storage of data

    C. Fast replication

    D. Regular backups offered by cloud providers

135. Which of the following methods can be used to attenuate the harm caused by the escalation of privilege?

    A. Extensive access control and authentication tools and techniques

    B. Analysis and review of all log data by trained, skilled personnel frequently

    C. Periodic and effective use of cryptographic sanitization tools

    D. The use of automated analysis tools such as SIM, SIEM, and SEM solutions

136. Which one of the following hypervisors would malicious attackers prefer to attack?

    A. Type 1

B. Type 2

C. Type 3

D. Type 4

137. Which term is used to define loss of access to data because the cloud provider has ceased operation?

A. Closing

B. Vendor lock-out

C. Vendor lock-in

D. Masking

138. Which vulnerabilities should always to be remembered when PaaS implementation is used for software development?

A. Malware

B. Loss/theft of portable devices

C. Backdoors

D. DoS/DDoS

139. Which levels have logical design for data separation to be incorporated?

A. Compute nodes and network

B. Storage nodes and application

C. Control plane and session

D. Management plane and presentation

140. What is the right name for Tier II of the Uptime Institute Data Center Site Infrastructure Tier Standard Topology?

A. Concurrently Maintainable Site Infrastructure

B. Fault-Tolerant Site Infrastructure

C. Basic Site Infrastructure

D. Redundant Site Infrastructure Capacity Components

141. Which of the ranges are recommended by the American Society of Heating, Refrigeration, and Air Conditioning Engineers (ASHRAE) for temperature and humidity in a data center?

   A. Between 62° F and 81° F and 40 percent and 65 percent relative humidity

   B. Between 64° F and 81° F and 40 percent and 60 percent relative humidity

   C. Between 64° F and 84° F and 30 percent and 60 percent relative humidity

   D. Between 60° F and 85° F and 40 percent and 60 percent relative humidity

142. Identify the right methods for iSCSI that are supported authentication.

   A. Kerberos

   B. TLS

   C. SRP

   D. L2TP

143. Which one of the followings is the primary challenge associated with the use of IPSec in a cloud computing environment?

   A. Access control and patch management

   B. Auditability and governance

   C. Configuration management and performance

   D. Training customers on how to use IPSec and documentation

144. Which option is suitable to mediate resource contention, when setting up resources shared within a host cluster?

   A. Reservations

   B. Limits

   C. Clusters

   D. Shares

145. Which items are disabled and which items remains enabled while using a maintenance mode?

   A. Customer access and alerts are disabled while logging remains enabled.

   B. Customer access and logging are disabled while alerts remain enabled.

    C. Logging and alerts are disabled while the ability to deploy new VMs remains enabled.

    D. Customer access and alerts are disabled while the ability to power on VMs remains enabled.

146. What are the most common service models in cloud computing?

    A. IaaS, DRaaS, and PaaS

    B. PaaS, SECaaS, and IaaS

    C. SaaS, PaaS, and IaaS

    D. Desktop as a service, PaaS, and IaaS

147. Identify the main characteristics of honeypot.

    A. Isolated, non-monitored environment

    B. Isolated, monitored environment

    C. Composed of virtualized infrastructure

    D. Composed of physical infrastructure

148. Which one of the following statements is related to the non-destructive testing (vulnerability assessment)?

    A. Detected vulnerabilities are not exploited during the vulnerability assessment.

    B. Known vulnerabilities are not exploited during the vulnerability assessment.

    C. Detected vulnerabilities are not exploited after the vulnerability assessment.

    D. Known vulnerabilities are not exploited before the vulnerability assessment.

149. Which of the followings is based on a physical network design created by CCSP, seeking to adopt good design practices and principles?

    A. A statement of work

    B. A series of interviews with stakeholders

    C. A design policy statement

    D. A logical network design

150. Identify the followings that has to be tied to with configuration management.

   A. Financial management

   B. Change management

   C. IT service management

   D. D Business relationship management

151. Which of the objectives is related to change management?

   A. Respond to a customer's changing business requirements while maximizing value and reducing incidents, disruption, and rework.

   B. Ensure that changes are recorded and evaluated.

   C. Respond to business, and IT requests for change that will disassociate services with business needs.

   D. Ensure that all changes are prioritized, planned, tested, implemented, documented, and reviewed in a controlled manner.

152. Which of the followings is the definition of an incident according to the ITIL framework?

   A. An unplanned interruption to an IT service or a reduction in the quality of an IT service

   B. A planned interruption to an IT service or a reduction in the quality of an IT service

   C. The unknown cause of one or more problems

   D. The identified root cause of a problem

153. Which of the followings are the differences between BC and BCM?

   A. BC is defined as the capability of the organization to continue the delivery of products or services at acceptable predefined levels following a disruptive incident. BCM is defined as a holistic management process that identifies actual threats to an organization and the impacts to business operations that those threats if realized, will cause. BCM provides a framework for building organizational resilience with the capability of an effective response that safeguards its key processes, reputation, brand, and value-creating activities.

   B. BC is defined as a holistic process that identifies potential threats to an organization and the impacts to business operations that those threats if realized,

might cause. BC provides a framework for building organizational resilience with the capability of an effective response that safeguards the interests of its key stakeholders, reputation, brand, and value-creating activities. BCM is defined as the capability of the organization to continue the delivery of products or services at acceptable predefined levels following a disruptive incident.

C. BC is defined as the capability of the first responder to continue delivery of products or services at acceptable predefined levels following a disruptive incident. BCM is defined as a holistic management process that identifies potential threats to an organization and the impacts to business operations that those threats if realized, will cause. BCM provides a framework for building organizational resilience with the capability of an effective response that safeguards the interests of its key stakeholders, reputation, brand, and value-creating activities.

D. BC is defined as the capability of the organization to continue the delivery of products or services at acceptable predefined levels following a disruptive incident. BCM is defined as a holistic management process that identifies potential threats to an organization and the impacts to business operations that those threats if realized, might cause. BCM provides a framework for building organizational resilience with the capability of an effective response that safeguards the interests of its key stakeholders, reputation, brand, and value-creating activities.

154. Which of the following steps are taken in the risk management process?
   A. Assessing, monitoring, transferring, and responding
   B. Framing, assessing, monitoring, and responding
   C. Framing, monitoring, documenting, and responding
   D. Monitoring, assessing, optimizing, and responding

155. Which of the followings is the evaluation of a risk assessment that is conducted by the organization?
   A. Threats to its assets, vulnerabilities not present in the environment, the likelihood that a threat will be realized by taking advantage of exposure, the impact that the exposure being realized will have on the organization and the residual risk

B. Threats to its assets, vulnerabilities present in the environment, the likelihood that a threat will be realized by taking advantage of exposure, the impact that the exposure being realized will have on another organization and the residual risk

C. Threats to its assets, vulnerabilities present in the environment, the likelihood that a threat will be realized by taking advantage of exposure, the impact that the exposure being realized will have on the organization and the residual risk

D. Threats to its assets, vulnerabilities present in the environment, the likelihood that a threat will be realized by taking advantage of exposure, the impact that the exposure being realized will have on the organization and the total risk

156. Which of the following are the minimum and customary practice of responsible protection of assets that affects a whole community and societal norm?

A. Due Diligence

B. Risk Mitigation

C. Asset Protection

D. Due Care

157. Which of the followings is the combination of risk within the realm of IT security?

A. Threat coupled with a breach

B. Threat coupled with a vulnerability

C. Vulnerability coupled with an attack

D. Threat coupled with a breach of security

158. Which of the followings is used to calculate an SLE?

A. Asset value and ARO

B. Asset value, LAFE, and SAFE

C. Asset value and exposure factor

D. LAFE and ARO

159. Identify the right process flow of digital forensics.

A. Identification of incident and evidence, analysis, collection, examination, and presentation

B. Identification of incident and evidence, examination, collection, analysis, and presentation

C. Identification of incident and evidence, collection, examination, analysis, and presentation

D. Identification of incident and evidence, collection, analysis, examination, and presentation

160. In which cloud service model, a customer is responsible for the administration of the OS?

    A. IaaS

    B. PaaS

    C. SaaS

    D. QaaS

161. Which of the followings might be offered by the cloud provider to address shared monitoring and testing responsibilities in a cloud configuration?

    A. Access to audit logs and performance data

    B. SIM, SEIM, and SEM logs

    C. DLP Solution Results

    D. Security Control Administration

162. Which mechanism should a customer use to ensure the complete trust in the provider's performance and duties, to whatever audit results that providers share with the customer?

    A. Statutes

    B. The contract

    C. Security control matrix

    D. HIPAA

163. Which type of SSAE audit report is a cloud customer most likely to receive from a cloud provider?

    A. SOC 1 Type 1

B. SOC 2 Type 2

C. SOC 1 Type 2

D. SOC 3

164. Which type of SSAE audit report is useful for a cloud customer, while it is unlikely that the cloud provider will share it?

A. SOC 1 Type 1

B. SOC 2 Type 2

C. SOC 1 Type 2

D. SOC 3

165. _____ was the Congressional response to some high-profile perfidy in several corporate cases, including WorldCom and Adelphia.

A. FERPA

B. GLBA

C. SOX

D. HIPAA

166. Which of the followings refer to the operating system hardening?

A. Limiting administrator access

B. Removing antimalware agents

C. Closing unused ports

D. Removing unnecessary services and libraries

167. Which of the followings can enhance the cloud customer(s) trust to the cloud provider?

A. Audits

B. Shared administration

C. Real-time video surveillance

D. SLAs

168. Which of the following ways that user access to the cloud environment can be administrated?

A. Customer directly administers access

B. Customer provides administration on behalf of the provider

C. Provider provides administration on behalf of the customer

D. The third party provides administration on behalf of the customer

169. Which type of SSAE audit reviews controls managing the organization(s) to control and assuring the confidentiality, integrity, and availability of data?

A. SOC 1

B. SOC 2

C. SOC 3

D. SOC 4

170. Which kind of SSAE report comes with a seal of approval from a certified auditor?

A. SOC 1

B. SOC 2

C. SOC 3

D. SOC 4

171. Which of the followings is a cloud provider likely to provide to its customers to improve the customer's trust in the provider?

A. Site visit access

B. SOC 2 Type 2

C. Audit and performance log data

D. Backend administrative access

172. Which of the following needs to be modify to deliver access to the customer in the cloud models?

A. Data

B. Security Controls

C. User Oermissions

D. OS

173. In all cloud models, which of the followings drive security controls?

A. Virtualization engine

B. Hypervisor

C. SLAs

D. Business requirements

174. In all cloud models, who will retain liability and responsibility for any data loss or disclosure?

A. Vendor

B. Customer

C. State

D. Administrator

175. Why will cloud providers be unlikely to allow physical access to their datacenters?

A. They want to enhance security by keeping information about physical layout and controls confidential.

B. They want to enhance exclusivity for their customers, so only an elite tier of higher paying clientele will be allowed physical access.

C. They want to minimize traffic in those areas, to maximize the efficiency of operational personnel.

D. Most data centers are inhospitable to human life, so minimizing physical access also minimizes safety concerns.

176. Many personnel are most likely to be reviewed; which type of software is this?

A. Database management software

B. Open source software

C. Secure software

D. Proprietary software

177. Which of the following techniques for controlling traffic can be used by the firewall?

A. Rule sets

B. Behavior analysis

C. Content filtering

D. Randomization

178. Which data has to be contained by honeypot?

A. Raw

B. Production

C. Useless

D. Sensitive

179. Which of the followings cannot be detect by the vulnerability assessment?

A. Malware

B. Defined vulnerabilities

C. Zero-day exploits

D. Programming flaws

180. When will data process be covered by the EU Data Protection Directive (Directive 95/46/EC)?

A. The directive applies to data processed by automated means and data contained in paper files.

B. The directive applies to data processed by a natural person in the course of purely personal activities.

C. The directive applies to data processed in the course of an activity that falls outside the scope of community law, such as public safety.

D. The directive applies to data processed by automated means in the course of purely personal activities.

181. Which of the following contractual components should be reviewed and fully understood by the CCSP when contracting with a CSP?

A. Concurrently maintainable site infrastructure

B. Use of subcontractors

C. Redundant site infrastructure capacity components

D. Scope of processing

182. What is an audit scope statement that provides a customer or organization with a cloud service?

A. The credentials of the auditors, as well as the projected cost of the audit

B. The required level of information for the client or organization subject to the audit to fully understand (and agree) with the scope, focus, and type of assessment being performed

C. A list of all the security controls to be audited

D. The outcome of the audit, as well as any findings that need to be addressed

183. Which of the followings should be performed first when a gap analysis is being performed?

A. Define scope and objectives

B. Identify potential risks

C. Obtain management support

D. Conduct information gathering

184. Which one is the first international set of cloud-based privacy controls?

A. ISO/IEC 27032

B. ISO/IEC 27005

C. ISO/IEC 27002

D. ISO/IEC 27018

185. What is domain A.16 of the ISO 27001:2013 standard?

A. Security Policy Management

B. Organizational Asset Management

C. System Security Management

D. Security Incident Management

186. What is the responsibility of a data custodian?

    A. The safe custody, transport, storage of data, and implementation of business rules

    B. Data content, context, and associated business rules

    C. Logging and alerts for all data

    D. Customer access and alerts for all data

187. What is usually not included in an SLA?

    A. Availability of the services to be covered by the SLA

    B. Change management process to be used

    C. Pricing for the services to be covered by the SLA

    D. Dispute mediation process to be used

188. Which of the followings best represents REST's definition?

    A. Built on protocol standards

    B. Lightweight and scalable

    C. Relies heavily on XML

    D. Only supports XML output

189. Which of the followings are the SDLC phases?

    A. Define

    B. Reject

    C. Design

    D. Test

190. Identify the components of the STRIDE model.

    A. Spoofing

    B. Repudiation

    C. Information disclosure

    D. External pen testing

191. Which one of the followings best describes SAST?

   A. A set of technologies that analyzes application source code, and bit code for coding and design problems that would indicate a security problem or vulnerability

   B. A set of technologies that analyzes application bit code, and binaries for coding and design problems that would indicate a security problem or vulnerability

   C. A set of technologies that analyzes application source code, byte code, and binaries for coding and design problems that would indicate a security problem or vulnerability

   D. A set of technologies that analyzes application source code for coding and design problems that would indicate a security problem or vulnerability

192. Which one of the followings best describes data masking?

   A. A method where the last few numbers in a dataset are not obscured. These are often used for authentication

   B. A method for creating similar but inauthentic datasets used for software testing and user training

   C. A method used to protect prying eyes from data such as social security numbers and credit card data

   D. Data masking involves stripping out all similar digits in a string of numbers to obscure the original number

193. Which one of the followings best describes a sandbox?

   A. An isolated space where transactions are protected from malicious software

   B. Space where you can safely execute malicious code to see what it does

   C. An isolated space where untested code and experimentation can safely occur separately from the production environment

   D. An isolated space where untested code and experimentation can safely occur within the production environment

194. Which of the followings ensures that the security discipline of Identity and Access Management (IAM) is correct?

   A. That all users are appropriately authorized

B. That the right individual gets access to the right resources at the right time for the right reasons

C. That all users are properly authenticated

D. That unauthorized users will get access to the right resources at the right time for the right reasons

195. Who is the identity provider and who is the reliant party in a federated identity arrangement using a trusted third party model?

A. A contracted third party/the various member organizations of the federation

B. The users of the various organizations within the federation/a CASB

C. Each member organization/a trusted third party

D. Each member organization/each member organization

196. Which one of the followings best describes the Organizational Normative Framework (ONF)?

A. A container for components of an application's security, best practices, cataloged and leveraged by the organization

B. A framework of containers for all components of application security, best practices, cataloged and leveraged by the organization

C. A set of application security, and best practices cataloged and leveraged by the organization

D. A framework of containers for some of the components of application security, best practices, cataloged and leveraged by the organization.

197. Which of the followings are defined by APIs?

A. A set of protocols, and tools for building software applications to access a web-based software application or tool

B. A set of standards for building software applications to access a web-based software application or tool

C. A set of routines, standards, protocols, and tools for building software applications to access a web-based software application or tool

D. A set of routines and tools for building software applications to access web-based software applications

198. Which one of the followings is the best description for the Application Normative Framework (ANF)?

    A. A stand-alone framework for storing security practices for the ONF

    B. A subset of the ONF

    C. A superset of the ONF

    D. The complete ONF

199. Which one of the followings is best described in SAML?

    A. A standard for developing secure application management logistics

    B. A standard for exchanging authentication and authorization data between security domains

    C. A standard for exchanging usernames and passwords across devices

    D. A standard used for directory synchronization

200. Which one of the followings best describes ISO/IEC 27034-1's purpose and scope?

    A. Describes international privacy standards for cloud computing

    B. Provides an overview of application security that introduces definitive concepts, principles, and processes involved in application security

    C. Serves as a newer replacement for NIST 800-53 r4

    D. Provides an overview of network and infrastructure security designed to secure cloud applications

201. Which one of the followings best describes data masking?

    A. Data masking is used in place of encryption for better performance

    B. Data masking is used to hide PII

    C. Data masking is used to create a similar, inauthentic dataset used for training and software testing

    D. Data masking is used in place of production data

202. What is a Database Activity Monitoring (DAM)?

    A. Host-based or network-based

B. Server-based or client-based

C. Used in the place of encryption

D. Used in place of data masking

203. Web Application Firewalls (WAFs) are primarily designed to protect applications against common attacks such as:

A. Syn floods

B. Ransomware

C. XSS and SQL injection

D. Password cracking

204. Which one of the followings best represents multifactor authentication?

A. A complex password and a secret code

B. Complex passwords and an HSM

C. A hardware token and a magnetic strip card

D. Something you know and something you have

205. SOAP is a protocol specification for the exchange of structured data or information in web services. Which of these is not right for SOAP?

A. Standards-based

B. Reliant on XML

C. Extremely fast

D. Works over numerous protocols

206. Which one of the followings is the best description of Dynamic Application Security Testing (DAST)?

A. Test performed on an application or software product while it is using real data in production

B. Test performed on an application or software product while it is being executed in memory in an operating system.

C. Test performed on an application or software product while being consumed by cloud customers

D. Masking

207. Which of the followings are the provisions by sandboxing?
  A. A test environment that isolates untrusted code changes for testing in a production environment
  B. A test environment that isolates untrusted code changes for testing in a nonproduction environment
  C. A testing environment where new and experimental code can be tested in a production environment
  D. A testing environment that prevents isolated code from running in a nonproduction environment

208. According to the Uptime Institute, which one is the lowest tier of data center redundancy?
  A. 1
  B. V
  C. C
  D. 4

209. According to the Uptime Institute, all tire perspective, which one is the actual amount of fuel that has to be on hand to power generators for backup data center power?
  A. 1
  B. 1,000 gallons
  C. 12 hours
  D. As much as needed to ensure all systems may be gracefully shut down and data securely stored

210. Which of the followings are the types of security training?
  A. Integral
  B. Initial
  C. Recurring

D. Refresher

211. Which one of the followings is a part of the STRIDE Model?

A. Repudiation

B. Redundancy

C. Resiliency

D. Rijndael

212. Which one of the followings is not a part of the STRIDE Model?

A. Spoofing

B. Tampering

C. Resiliency

D. Information disclosure

213. Which one of the following is not a feature of SAST?

A. Source code review

B. Team-building efforts

C. "White-box" testing

D. Highly skilled, often expensive outside consultants

214. Which one of the followings is not a feature of DAST?

A. Testing in runtime

B. User teams performing executable testing

C. "Black-box" testing

D. Binary inspection

215. Which one of the followings is not the feature of secure KVM components?

A. Keystroke logging

B. Sealed exterior case

C. Welded chipsets

D. Push-button selectors

216. What redundancy can we expect to find in a data center in any tier?

    A. All operational components

    B. All infrastructure

    C. Emergency egress

    D. Full power capabilities

217. What should be the primary focus of redundancy and contingency planning in data centers?

    A. Critical path/operations

    B. Health and human safety

    C. Infrastructure supporting the production environment

    D. Power and HVAC

218. Which of the following technologies uses parities and disk striping to ensure the cloud's datacenter storage resilience?

    A. Cloud-bursting

    B. RAID

    C. Data dispersion

    D. SAN

219. During contingency operations, which one of the following resiliency techniques attenuates the possible loss of functional capabilities?

    A. Cross-training

    B. Metered usage

    C. Proper placement of HVAC temperature measurements tools

    D. Raised floors

220. Which one of the followings is not the attribute as the cause of lost capabilities due to DoS?

    A. Hackers

B. Construction equipment

C. Changing regulatory motif

D. Squirrels

221. Which one of the followings helps in the ability to demonstrate due diligence efforts?

A. Redundant power lines

B. HVAC placement

C. Security training documentation

D. Bollards

222. Which one of the followings is a primary challenge to getting both redundant power and communications utility connections?

A. Expense

B. Carrying medium

C. Personnel deployment

D. Location of many datacenters

223. Which one of the followings is not a component of physical security that should to be considered in the planning and design of a cloud data center facility?

A. Perimeter

B. Vehicular approach/traffic

C. Fire suppression

D. Elevation of dropped ceilings

224. Which of the followings is also known as the Brewer-Nash Security Model?

A. MAC

B. The Chinese Wall model

C. Preventive measures

D. RBAC

225. What type of hypervisor would malicious actors prefer attacking as it offers a more significant area of attack?

    A. Cat IV

    B. Type II

    C. Bare metal

    D. Converged

226. Which of the following techniques ensures the resilience of cloud data centers use encrypted data chunks?

    A. Cloud-bursting

    B. RAID

    C. Data dispersion

    D. SAN

227. The most effective form of BC / DR testing is:

    A. Tabletop

    B. Dry run

    C. Full test

    D. Structured test

228. What type of BC / DR testing has the least effect on operations?

    A. Tabletop

    B. Dry run

    C. Full test

    D. Structured test

229. What characteristic of liquid propane enhances its desirability as fuel for backup generators?

    A. Burn rate

    B. Price

    C. Does not spoil

D. Flavor

230. Adherence to ASHRAE humidity standards can minimize the possibility of _____.

    A. Breach

    B. Static discharge

    C. Theft

    D. Inversion

231. How long does the backup provided by UPS last?

    A. 12 hours

    B. 10 minutes

    C. One day

    D. Long enough for graceful shutdown

232. In what time frame should a generator transfer switch put backup power online?

    A. 10 seconds

    B. Before the recovery point objective is reached

    C. Before the UPS duration is exceeded

    D. Three days

233. What is the automatic patching characteristic?

    A. Cost

    B. Speed

    C. Noise reduction

    D. Capability to recognize problems quickly

234. What tool can minimize confusion and misunderstanding when a BC/DR responds?

    A. Flashlight

    B. Controls matrix

    C. Checklist

D. Call tree

235. Which of the following stakeholders include in the CMB?
   A. Regulators
   B. IT department
   C. Security office
   D. Management

236. Which of the followings is included in the OS monitoring for performance perspective?
   A. Disk space
   B. Disk I/O usage
   C. CPU usage
   D. Print spooling

237. Which of the following actions requires the maintenance mode?
   A. Remove all active production instances
   B. Initiate enhanced security controls
   C. Prevent new logins
   D. Ensure logging continues

238. Which capability is offered by the UPS, in addition to a battery backup?
   A. Communication redundancy
   B. Line conditioning
   C. Breach alert
   D. Confidentiality

239. Deviations from the baselines have to be investigated and _____.
   A. Documented
   B. Enforced
   C. Revealed

D. Encouraged

240. Which of the followings should be covered by baseline?
   A. As many systems throughout the organization as possible
   B. Data breach alerting and reporting
   C. A process for version control
   D. All regulatory compliance requirements

241. Which one of the followings is used in a cost-effective manner to be addressed by the localized incident or disaster?
   A. UPS
   B. Generators
   C. Joint operating agreements
   D. Strict adherence to applicable regulations

242. What is the minimum time to take a generator fuel storage for a cloud data center?
   A. 10 minutes
   B. Three days
   C. Indefinitely
   D. 12 hours

243. Which of the followings should be included by the BC/DR kit?
   A. Flashlight
   B. Documentation equipment
   C. Hard drives
   D. Annotated asset inventory

244. Which one is the least changing about eDiscovery in the cloud?
   A. Decentralization of data storage
   B. Complexities of International law
   C. Identifying roles such as data owner, controller, and processor

    D. Forensic analysis

245. Which of the followings refer by the Legal controls?

    A. Controls designed to comply with laws and regulations related to the cloud environment

    B. PCI DSS

    C. ISO 27001

    D. NIST 800-53r4

246. Which one of the followings is not associated with cloud forensics?

    A. Analysis

    B. eDiscovery

    C. Chain of custody

    D. Plausibility

247. Which one of the followings is not a part of contractual PII?

    A. Scope of processing

    B. Use of subcontractors

    C. Location of data

    D. Value of data

248. Which one of the followings is the best example of the main component of regulated PII?

    A. Items that should be implemented

    B. Mandatory breach reporting

    C. Audit rights of subcontractors

    D. PCI DSS

249. Which one of the following is not associated with security?

    A. Confidentiality

    B. Availability

C. Integrity

D. Quality

250. Which one of the following is the superior benefit of an external audit?

A. Independence

B. Oversight

C. Cheaper

D. Better results

251. In audit practices, which one is the law resulted from a lack of independence?

A. HIPAA

B. GLBA

C. SOX

D. ISO 27064

252. Which one of the followings are the obsolete report types?

A. SAS 70

B. SSAE 16

C. SOC 1

D. SOC 3

253. Which one of the followings is the most aligned report with financial control audits?

A. SOC 1

B. SOC 2

C. SOC 3

D. SSAE 16

254. What is the objective of a SOC 3 report?

A. Absolute assurances

B. Compliance with PCI/DSS

C. HIPAA compliance

D. Seal of approval

255. What is the objective of gap analysis performance?
   A. To begin the benchmarking process
   B. To provide assurances to cloud customers
   C. To assure proper accounting practices are being used
   D. To ensure all controls are in place and working properly

256. Which organization are created and maintained by the GAAPs?
   A. ISO
   B. ISO/IEC
   C. PCI Council
   D. AICPA

257. In the financial industry, which law addresses security and privacy matters?
   A. GLBA
   B. FERPA
   C. SOX
   D. HIPAA

258. Which one of the followings is not the example of a highly regulated environment?
   A. Healthcare
   B. Financial services
   C. Wholesale or distribution
   D. Public companies

259. Which one of the followings is the SOC report subtypes addressing a point in time?
   A. SOC 2
   B. Type I
   C. Type II
   D. SOC 3

260. Which one of the SOC report subtypes spans a period?
    A. SOC 2
    B. SOC 3
    C. SOC 1
    D. Type II

261. Which of the followings refers to the right to be forgotten?
    A. The right to no longer pay taxes
    B. Erasing criminal history
    C. The right to have all of a data owner's data erased
    D. Masking

262. Which of the following documents should be a part of a right to audit?
    A. SLA
    B. PLA
    C. All cloud providers
    D. Masking

263. Which of the following was enacted the SOX?
    A. Poor BOD oversight
    B. Lack of independent audits
    C. Poor financial controls
    D. All of the above

264. Identify the component of GLBA.
    A. The right to be forgotten
    B. EU Data Directives
    C. The information security program
    D. The right to audit

265. Which one of the followings is not related to the HIPAA controls?

    A. Administrative controls

    B. Technical controls

    C. Physical controls

    D. Financial controls

266. What does the doctrine of the proper law refer to?

    A. How jurisdictional disputes are settled

    B. The law that is applied after the first law is applied

    C. The determination of what law will apply to a case

    D. The proper handling of eDiscovery materials

267. Which of the followings refer to the Restatement (Second) Conflict of Law?

    A. The basis for deciding which laws are most appropriate in a situation where conflicting laws exist

    B. When judges restate the law in an opinion

    C. How jurisdictional disputes are settled

    D. Whether local or federal laws apply in a situation

268. What are the characteristics of Stored Communications Act (SCA)?

    A. It is old

    B. It is in bad need of updating

    C. It is unclear about current technologies

    D. All of the above

269. Which one of the followings is the lowest level of the CSA STAR program?

    A. Continuous monitoring

    B. Self-assessment

    C. Hybridization

    D. Attestation

270. Which one of the followings is a valid risk management metric?

    A. KPI

    B. KRI

    C. SLA

    D. SOC

271. Which frameworks focus on design implementation and management?

    A. ISO 31000:2009

    B. HIPAA

    C. ISO 27017

    D. NIST 800-92

272. Which frameworks find the top eight security risks based on likelihood and impact?

    A. NIST 800-53

    B. ISO 27000

    C. ENISA

    D. COBIT

273. Identify the levels of CSA STAR program.

    A. Self-assessment

    B. Third-party assessment-based certification

    C. SOC 2 audit certification

    D. Continuous monitoring–based certification

274. Which is ISO standard addressing security risk in a supply chain?

    A. ISO 27001

    B. ISO/IEC 28000:2007

    C. ISO 18799

    D. ISO 31000:2009

275. Identify risk management frameworks.

    A. NIST SP 800-37

    B. European Union Agency for Network and Information Security (ENISA)

    C. Key risk indicators (KRI)

    D. ISO 31000:2009

276. Which one of the followings is the best defined risk?

    A. Threat coupled with a breach

    B. Vulnerability coupled with an attack

    C. Threat coupled with a threat actor

    D. Threat coupled with a vulnerability

277. Which one of the followings is not a component of the ENISA Top 8 Security Risks of cloud computing?

    A. Vendor lock-in

    B. Isolation failure

    C. Insecure or incomplete data deletion

    D. Availability

278. Which one of the followings is a risk management way that halts a business function?

    A. Mitigation

    B. Acceptance

    C. Transference

    D. Avoidance

279. Which one of the followings is best to describe a cloud carrier?

    A. A person or entity responsible for making a cloud service available to consumers

    B. The intermediary who provides connectivity and transport of cloud services between cloud providers and cloud consumers

    C. The person or entity responsible for keeping cloud services running for customers

D. The person or entity responsible for transporting data across the Internet

280. Which method of risk is associated with insurance?
    A. Transference
    B. Avoidance
    C. Acceptance
    D. Mitigation

281. Which of the following components are part of a CCSP and should be reviewed when looking at contracting with a cloud service provider?
    A. The physical layout of the datacenter
    B. Background checks for the provider's personnel
    C. Use of subcontractors
    D. Redundant uplink grafts

282. Data custodian is responsible for _____.
    A. The safe custody, transport, storage of the data, and implementation of business rules
    B. Logging access and alerts
    C. Data content
    D. Data context

283. Which one of the following is not a term to manage risk?
    A. Enveloping
    B. Mitigating
    C. Accepting
    D. Transferring

284. Which one of the followings is not a risk management framework?
    A. Hex GBL
    B. COBIT

C. NIST SP 800-37

D. ISO 31000:2009

285. Which one of the followings is not appropriate to include in an SLA?

A. The number of user accounts allowed during a specified period

B. Which personnel are responsible and authorized between both the provider and the customer to declare an emergency and transition the service to a contingency operation status

C. The amount of data allowed to be transmitted and received between the cloud provider and customer

D. The time allowed migrating from normal operations to contingency operations

286. Which one of the followings is the best to description of a Cloud Security Alliance Cloud Controls Matrix (CCM)?

A. An inventory of cloud service security controls that are arranged into separate security domains

B. An inventory of cloud services security controls that are arranged into a hierarchy of security domains

C. A set of regulatory requirements for cloud service providers

D. A set of software development life cycle requirements for cloud service providers

287. Which one of the followings is not a type of controls?

A. Transitional

B. Administrative

C. Technical

D. Physical

288. Which one of the followings is not an example of an essential stakeholder?

A. IT analyst

B. IT director

C. CFO

D. HR director

Answers:

Answers

1. D
Explanation: The most common cloud service models are:
- Infrastructure as a Service (IaaS)
- Software as a Service (SaaS)
- Platform as a Service (PaaS)

2. A, B and C
Explanation: Virtualization enables scalable resource allocation; broadband connections enable users to have remote access from anywhere, anytime; cryptographic connections enable secure remote access.

3. A.
Explanation: Service-Level Agreements (SLAs) specify goal measures that describe what the cloud provider will offer to the customer.

4. D.
Explanation: Availability issue is the main reason behind the lack of access to the customer.

5. A, C and D
Explanation: Cloud Access Security Brokers (CASBs) offer independent identity and access management (IAM) services to the customers and the CSP. They offer several services including single sign-on, certificate management, and cryptographic key escrow.

6. D
Explanation: Magnetic swipe card data is usually not encrypted.

7. B
Explanation: Moving an application to the cloud may or may not be reduced, because it depends on your situation and application before moving into the cloud.

8. B
Explanation: Backup is still as relevant as always, regardless of where your primary data and backups are stored.

9. B
Explanation: There are no written laws that a cloud customer needs to remain with a particular cloud provider.

10. B.
Explanation: This is the definition of vendor lock-out.

11. A, C and D
Explanation: Reversed charging configuration does not feature cloud computing as others are.

12. C
Explanation: The data owner is responsible for any breaches that result in unauthorized disclosure of PII, under the law; this includes breaches caused by contracted parties and outsources services. The data owner is the cloud customer.

13. B
Explanation: The Business Impact Analysis (BIA) is designed to signify the value of the organization's assets, and learn the critical paths and processes.

14. A
Explanation:
A virtual private cloud is an on-demand configurable pool of shared computing resources allocated within a public cloud environment, providing a certain level of isolation between the different organizations using the resources.
On-Premise Private Cloud. On-Premise Private Cloud, often called Internal Cloud, is hosted within an organizations own offices, or data center, and provides an internal solution for hosting needs.

15. B
Explanation: The public cloud is defined as computing services offered by third-party providers over the public Internet, making them available to anyone who wants to use or purchase them. They may be free or sold on-demand, allowing customers to pay only per usage for the CPU cycles, storage, or bandwidth they consume.

16. D
Explanation: Community cloud deployment model provides a joint ownership of assets between an affinity group.

17. B
Explanation: PaaS enables the cloud customer to install a variety of software, including software to be tested.

18. C
Explanation: SaaS is the cloud service model that is proving a cloud customer to do little maintenances and some necessary administration tasks.

19. A

Explanation: IaaS provides a hot or warm DR site, with hardware, connectivity, and utilities, allowing the customer to build out any type of software configuration.

20. A

Explanation: NIST Define the definition of Cloud Computing:

"Cloud computing is a model for enabling ubiquitous, convenient, on-demand network access to a shared pool of configurable computing resources (e.g., networks, servers, applications, and services) that can be rapidly provisioned and released with minimal management effort or service provider interaction".

21. D

Explanation: According to the MSP Alliance, typically MSPs have the following distinguishing characteristics:

- Have some form of NOC service
- Have some form of help desk service
- Can remotely monitor and manage all or a majority of the objects for the customer
- Can proactively maintain the objects under management for the customer
- Can deliver these solutions with some form of predictable billing model, where the customer knows with high accuracy what her regular IT management expense will be

22. B

Explanation: **CSP:** An organization that provides a cloud-based platform, infrastructure, application, or storage services to the other organizations or individuals typically charge a fess; otherwise known to clients "as a service".

Cloud Backup Service Provider: A third-party entity that handles and contains operational responsibilities for cloud-based data backup services and solutions to customers from a central data center.

23. A and D

Explanation: The NIST defines the Cloud Computing essential characteristics are as follows:

- **On-demand Self-Service**: A customer can individually provision computing capabilities, such as network storage and server time, as needed automatically without requiring human interaction with each service provider.
- **Broad Network Access**: Capabilities are available over the network and accessed through standard mechanisms that promote use by heterogeneous thin or thick client platforms (such as mobile phones, tablets, laptops, and workstations).

24. C

Explanation: The main building blocks of cloud computing are RAM, CPU, storage, and networking.

25. D

Explanation: NIST defines Cloud Computing in IaaS:

"The capability provided to the consumer is to provision processing, storage, networks, and other fundamental computing resources where the consumer can deploy and run arbitrary software, which

can include operating systems and applications. The consumer does not manage or control the underlying cloud infrastructure but has control over operating systems, storage, and deployed applications; and possibly limited control of select networking components (e.g., host firewalls)".

26. A
Explanation: IaaS has many critical benefits for organizations, which include but are not limited to the following:

- Usage metered and priced based on units consumed. This can be billed back to specific departments or functions as well
- The ability to scale up and down infrastructure services based on actual usage
- This is particularly useful and beneficial when there are significant spikes and dips within the usage curve for infrastructure
- Minimize the cost of ownership. There is no need to buy assets for everyday use, no loss of asset value over time, and minimize costs of maintenance and support
- Minimize energy and cooling costs along with "green IT" environment effect with optimum use of IT resources and systems

27. C
Explanation: NIST defines Cloud Computing, in PaaS:
"The capability provided to the consumer is to deploy onto the cloud infrastructure consumer-created or acquired applications created using programming languages, libraries, services, and tools supported by the provider. The consumer does not manage or control the basic cloud infrastructure including network, servers, operating systems, or storage, but has control over the deployed applications and possibly configuration settings for the application-hosting environment".

28. B
Explanation: PaaS has to contain the following characteristics and advantages:

- Support multiple languages and frameworks
- Multiple hosting environments
- Flexibility
- Allow choice and reduce lock-in
- Ability to auto-scale

29. A
Explanation: NIST defines Cloud Computing, in SaaS:
"*The capability provided to the consumer is to use the provider's applications running on a cloud infrastructure. The applications are accessible from various client devices through either a thin client interface, such as a web browser (e.g., web-based e-mail), or a program interface. The consumer does not manage or control the underlying cloud infrastructure including network, servers, operating systems, storage, or even individual application capabilities, with the possible exception of limited user-specific application configuration settings*".

30. D

Explanation: NIST defines cloud computing; the cloud deployments models are as follows:

- Public
- Private
- Hybrid
- Community

31. B

Explanation: As with systems and other organizational assets, data has a contained and managed lifecycle across the following key stages:
Create, archive, use, share, store, and destroy.

32. C

Explanation:

- **SOC 1:** A report on controls at a service organization that may be relevant to a user entity's internal control over financial reporting
- **SOC 2:** This report is based on the existing SysTrust and WebTrust principles. The purpose of a SOC 2 report is to evaluate an organization's information systems relevant to security, availability, processing integrity, confidentiality, or privacy.
- **SOC 3:** This report is also based on the existing SysTrust and WebTrust principles, like a SOC 2 report. The difference is that the SOC 3 report does not detail the testing performed

33. A

Explanation: SOC 2 reporting was specially designed for IT-managed service providers and cloud computing. The report specially identified the main Trust Services principles, which are as follows:
Security, Availability, Processing Integrity, Confidentiality, and Privacy.

34. D

Explanation: PaaS security concerns are:

- System and Resource Isolations
- User Level Permissions
- User Access Management
- Protection Against Malware/ Backdoors/ Trojans

35. B

Explanation: When we gather information about business requirements, we must do a complete inventory, receive an accurate valuation of assets (usually from the owners of those assets), and assess criticality; this collection of information does not tell us, objectively, how useful an asset is, however.

36. A, C and D

Explanation: The BIA can be used to provide information in the risk assessment, the selection of specific security controls throughout the environment, and the Business Continuity/Disaster Recovery plan(s) (BC/DR); knowing the critical aspects of the organization and the values of all assets is essential to accomplishing these tasks.

37. D
Explanation: The service of IaaS is bare metal, and the customer has to install the OS and the software; the customer then is responsible for maintaining that OS.

38. C
Explanation: In PaaS, the provider supplies the hardware, connectivity, and OS; the customer installs and maintains applications.

39. A
Explanation: A customer is supplied only the data in the SaaS service model. So, the customer is responsible for the data.

40. B
Explanation: The contract codifies the rights and responsibilities of the parties involved upon completion of negotiation.

41. D
Explanation: Layered defense calls for a diverse approach to security.

42. B, C, and D
Explanation:
- Keystroke logging is a technical control
- door locks are a physical control
- biometric authentication is a technological control.

So, this option is not considered an administrative control, but Access Control process is considered an Administrative Control.

43. B, C, and D
Explanation: The safe and extinguisher are physical control, and firing someone is an administrative control. So, these options are not considered as a technological control. However, the firewall is a technological control.

44. D
Explanation: Fences are physical controls; carpets and ceilings are architectural features, and a door is not necessarily control.

45. D

Explanation: All of these activities have to involve in the encryption, except for profile formatting, which is a made-up term.

46. B, C, and D
Explanation: All these options are involved in the process of hardening devices except for "improve default account". Moreover, we do not want to improve default accounts—we want to remove them.

47. A, C and D
Explanation:

- Encrypting the OS is a distractor
- Video cameras are security control
- Background checks are good for vetting personnel

So, All these options are not involved in the process of hardening a device except updating and patching the system helps harden the system.

48. A
Explanation: Homomorphic encryption has to accomplish that objective.

49. B
Explanation: In the organization, senior management decides the risk appetite.

50. C
Explanation: The residual risk is the amount of risk or danger associated with an action or event remaining after natural or inherent risks have been reduced by risk controls..

51. A, C and D
Explanation: These options are addressing risks except reversal is not a method for handling risk.

52. A, B and C
Explanation: All these options are ways to harden a mobile device except "two-person integrity" is a concept that has nothing to do with the topic, and, if implemented, would require everyone in your organization to walk around in pairs while using their mobile devices.

53. A, B and C
Explanation: These options are good tactics for securing devices except removing all admin accounts; we cannot remove all admin accounts; the device will need to be administered at some point, and that account needs to be there.

54. C
Explanation: The potential for loss, damage or destruction of an asset as a result of a threat exploiting a vulnerability. Risk is the intersection of assets, threats, and vulnerabilities.

55. B

Explanation: To determine the necessary controls to be deployed, you need to understand function(s) and location(s) of the data and actor(s) upon the data.

56. D
Explanation: IaaS uses the following storage types:
- Volume and object

57. B
Explanation: PaaS uses the following storage types:
- Structured and Unstructured

58. A and C
Explanation: Encryption preventing unauthorized data viewing while masking refers to the different alternatives for the protection of data without encryption.

59. C
Explanation: Data loss prevention tool implementations typically conform the following topologies:
- Data in Motion (DIM)
- Data at Rest (DAR)
- Data in Use (DAU)

DIM is referred to as a network-based or gateway DLP. In this topology, the monitoring engine is deployed near the organizational gateway to monitor outgoing protocols such as HTTP/HTTPS/SMTP and FTP.

60. D
Explanation: For database encryption, you need to understand the following options:
- File-level encryption
- Transparent encryption
- Application-level encryption

Various DBMS contain the ability to encrypt the whole database or specific parts, such as tables. The encryption engine resides within the database; it is transparent to the application.

61. A
Explanation: Data discovery tools differ by technique and data matching abilities. There are three main analysis methods are metadata, label, and content analysis.

62. C
Explanation: Where community or national laws or regulations determine the objcetives and means of processing, the controller or the particular criteria for this nomination may be designated by the community or national law.

63. B

Explanation: The Cloud Security Alliance Cloud Controls Matrix (CCM) is the most important and newly security controls framework that is addressed to the stakeholders and cloud community. CCM is capable of providing mapping or cross relationships with the main industry-accepted security standards, regulations, and controls frameworks such as the ISO 27001/27002, ISACA's COBIT, and PCI-DSS.

64. A
Explanation: The most common capabilities of information rights management solutions are:
- Persistent protection
- Dynamic policy control
- Automatic expiration
- Continuous audit trail, and
- Support for existing authentication infrastructure

65. D
Explanation: An organization's established protocol for retaining information for operational or regulatory compliance needs is called a data retention policy. This policy has to define retention periods, data formats, data security, and data retrieval procedures for the organization.

66. B
Explanation: To safely dispose of electronic records, the following options are available:
- Physical destruction
- Encryption
- Overwriting
- Degaussing
- Crypto-shredding

While using an encryption method to rewrite the data in an encrypted format to make it unreadable without the encryption key.

67. C
Explanation: The following principles have to be adopted as part of the security operations policies to support continuous operations.
- Audit logging
- Contract/authority maintenance
- Secure disposal
- Incident response legal preparation

While the continuous operation of audit logging is comprised of three important processes are detecting new events, adding new rules, and reducing false positive.

68. A, C, and D
Explanation: There are three primary data discovery methods that are employed:
- Metadata, Labels, and Content analysis

69. C
Explanation: This option might be included in data labels.

70. A, B, and C
Explanation: These are data analytics methods except refractory iterations.

71. A, B, and D
Explanation: These might be included in data labels except the delivery vendor.

72. B
Explanation: In a cloud configuration, cloud customer is usually considered as the data owner; The data in question is the customer's data that is to be processed in the cloud.

73. A, B, and C
Explanation: These options might be included in data labels except multifactor authentication.

74. C
Explanation: Data processor is referred to anyone who stores, handles, moves, or manipulates data on behalf of the data owner or controller. In the cloud computing realm, this is the cloud provider. This definition applies only in the legal way.

75. A
Explanation: Policy drives contain all programs and functions in the organization; the organization does not need to perform any operations that do not have a policy governing them.

76. A, B, and C
Explanation: These options organization should include in the policies except Policy adjudication.

77. B
Explanation: Crypto-shredding is the only reasonable alternative. Other options are not suitable for data disposal perspective.

78. A
Explanation: This option is suitable for intellectual property protection. Copyrights are protected tangible expressions of creative works.

79. B
Explanation: Patents protect processes (as well as inventions, new plant life, and decorative patterns).

80. D

Explanation: Trade secrets is related to intellectual property protection for a precious set of sales leads. Marketing materials and private sales rare to the organization are trade secrets.

81. D
Explanation: Trade secrets option is suitable for intellectual property protection for a secret recipe for muffins. Confidential recipes are unique to the organization that is trade secrets.

82. C
Explanation: Logos, symbols, phrases and color schemes are described brands to the trademarks.

83. C
Explanation: Take down notice aspect related to the DMCA while the DMCA provision for takedown notices enables copyright holders to demand eliminate of suspect content from the web, and puts the burden of proof on whoever posted the material.

84. B
Explanation: The United States Patent and Trademark Office (USPTO) accepts, reviews, and approves applications for new patents.

85. A, B, and C
Explanation: All these option that can be included. DRM solutions use all these methods except for dip switch validity.

86. A, B, and C
Explanation: Asia, Europe, and South America regions have at least one country with an overarching, federal privacy law protecting personal data of its citizens. All EU member countries follow the Data Protection Regulation. Argentina's Personal Data Protection Act cleaves to the EU Regulation, as does Japan's Act on the Protection of Personal Information.

87. A, C, and D
Explanation: Persistency, Automatic expiration, and Dynamic policy control should include DRM solutions as a function.

88. B
Explanation: According to NIST's Cloud Computing Synopsis and Recommendations:
"Cloud carrier is an intermediary that provides connectivity and transport of cloud services between CSPs and cloud consumers".

89. A and D
Explanation: According to **OpenNetworking.org**, software-based networking is defined as the physical separation of the network control plane from the forwarding plane, and where a control plane manages various devices.

This architecture decouples the network control and forwarding functions, thus allowing the network control to become directly programmable and the underlying infrastructure to be abstracted for applications and network services. The SDN architecture has the following characteristics:

- Directly Programmable
- Agile
- Centrally managed
- Programmatically configured
- Open standards-based and vendor neutral

While network control is directly programmable because it is decoupled from forwarding functions and when implemented through open standards, SDN simplifies network design and operation.

90. B

Explanation: The use of limits, reservations, and shares delivers the dependent ability for an administrator to allocate the computing resources of a host. A reservation set up a guaranteed minimum resource allocation that needs to be met by the host with physical compute resources to enable a guest to power on and operate. This reservation is usually available for CPU and even RAM as well, or both, or as required. A limit set up the highest ceiling for resource allocation. This ceiling may be fixed, or it may be expandable, permitting for the acquisition of more compute resources through a borrowing scheme from the root resource provider.

91. A

Explanation: The main problem that the CCSP should understand is data consistency of object storage systems is accomplished only eventually. When you update a file, you may have to wait until the change is propagated to all the copies before requests return the latest version. This makes object storage unsuitable for data that changes frequently.

92. C

Explanation: Even though other risks might not seem to be in virtualized environments because of choices made by the architect, implementer, and customer, virtualization risks usually are seen as including the following:

- Guest breakout
- Snapshot and image security
- Sprawl

93. D

Explanation: Implementation of controls needs cooperation and a clear demarcation of responsibility between the CSP and the cloud consumer. Without that, there is an actual risk for specific significant controls to be absent.

94. B and C

Explanation: There are some examples of trust zones that can include demilitarized zones (DMZs); site-specific zones, such as segmentation according to department or function; and application defined zones, such as the three tiers of a web application.

95. C

Explanation: Cloud infrastructures have most characteristics that can be distinct advantages in realizing BCDR, depending on the case:

- Rapid elasticity
- Broad network connectivity
- A pay-per-use model

96. A, C, and D

Explanation: These terms are the methods of obscuring data except data discovery.

97. A, B, and C

Explanation: Goals of SIEM implementation include the followings:

- Centralize Collection of Log Data
- Enhanced Analysis Capabilities
- Dashboarding
- Automated Response

98. A, C, and D

Explanation: Like SIEM, DLP solutions generally have various significant goals:

- Additional Security
- Policy Enforcement
- Enhanced Monitoring
- Regulatory Compliance

99. C

Explanation: We can process data in the cloud while it is encrypted, without having to decrypt it. Although this capability is not currently available, ongoing research shows promise. This technology is known as homomorphic encryption, and it is worth knowing the term and understanding the possibility, even though it is still in the experimental stages.

100. A

Explanation: DLP tools must be understood to know which information to monitor and which needs categorization and this is usually done upon data creation, by the data owners.

101. A

Explanation: To implement tokenization, there will need to be two databases: the database containing the raw, actual data, and the token database containing tokens that map to actual data.

102. A, B, and C

Explanation: Data masking can be used to provide all of the following functionality:

- Secure remote access

- Enforcing the least privilege
- Test data in sandboxed environments

103. A
Explanation: DRM can be combined with DLP to secure intellectual property; both are managing data that fall into particular categories by default.

104. B
Explanation: EAR is a Commerce Department program. Evaluation Assurance Levels (EAR) are intellectual part of the Common Criteria standard from ISO. Digital Rights Management (DRM) tools are used for protecting electronic processing of intellectual property.

105. A
Explanation: ITAR is a Department of State program. EAR is an intellectual part of the Common Criteria standard from ISO. DRM tools are used for protecting electronic processing of intellectual property.

106. B
Explanation: Cryptographic keys should not be stored along with the data they secure, regardless of key length.

107. A, B, and C
Explanation: All of these options are the best practices of crucial management except multifactor authentication.

108. A
Explanation: The best answer to this question is "**To a level at least as high as the data they can decrypt**", because it is always true, whereas the remaining options depend on circumstances.

109. A, B, and C
Explanation: All of these options have to be considered when creating archival data policies, except Immediacy of the technology.

110. B
Explanation: The correct order of the data life cycle is:

- Create
- Store
- Use
- Share
- Archive
- Destroy

111. B
Explanation: Cloud Access Security Broker (CASB) is a third-party entity to providing independent identity and access management (IAM) services to CSPs and cloud customers, often as an intermediary.

112. B
Explanation: The data is stored and displayed as with a file structure in the legacy environment, as files and folders, with all the same hierarchical and naming functions is known as File-Based Storage.

113. D
Explanation: A form of data caching, typically near geophysical locations of high user demand, for copies of data commonly requested by users is known as Content Delivery Network (CDN).

114. B
Explanation: APIs can be broken into multiple formats; most commonly are REST and SOAP. While REST is a software architecture style of best practice and guidelines for developing scalable web services.

115. A
Explanation: There are following phases of software development lifecycle model that are:
- Planning and requirements analysis
- Defining
- Designing
- Developing
- Testing

116. B
Explanation: **"Whenever an application takes untrusted data and sends it to a web browser without proper validation or escaping"** that situation is meet the XSS flaws in the application, so the security analyst identify that attack is an XSS attack.

117. C
Explanation: In a federated environment, there is a relying party and an identity provider. The relying party is the service provider and consumes these tokens. The identity provider holds all the identities and generates a token for known users.

118. D
Explanation: ISO/IEC 27034-1 defines an **Application Security Management Process (ASMP)** to manage and maintain each an **Application Normative Framework (ANF)**. The ASMP is created in five steps:
1. Specifying the application requirements and environment
2. Assessing application security risks
3. Creating and maintaining the ANF

4. Provisioning and operating the application
5. Auditing the security of the application

119. D
Explanation: Cloud Portability is the ability to move applications and associated data between one cloud provider and another, or between legacy and cloud environments.

120. A, B, and C
Explanation: There are three general means of using cloud backups for BC/DR. The primary ways of using cloud backups for BC/DR include the following:
- Private Architecture, Cloud Service as Backup
- Cloud Operations, Cloud Provider as Backup
- Cloud Operations, Third-Party Cloud Backup Provider

121. A, C, D
Explanation: The following countermeasures are taken for protecting cloud operations against external attackers are:
- Continual monitoring for anomalous activity
- Hardened devices and systems, including servers, hosts, hypervisors, and virtual machines
- Regular and detailed configuration/change management activities.

122. A, B, and C
Explanation: There are many things an organization can do to enhance the portability of its data:
- Ensure favorable contract terms for portability
- Avoid proprietary formats
- Ensure there are no physical limitations to moving

123. B, C, and D
Explanation:
- Dual control is not useful for remote access devices, because we would have to assign two people for every device, which would decrease efficiency and productivity
- Muddling is a cocktail preparation technique that involves crushing ingredients
- Safe Harbor is a policy provision that allows for compliance through an alternate method than the primary instruction

124. A, B, and C
Explanation: Your data and operations will be dependent on external parties in entirely new ways after migration. Not only will you have to depend on the cloud provider to meet your organization's needs, but all the downstream and upstream dependencies associated with the provider as well, including the provider's vendors, suppliers, utilities, personnel, and so on.

125. A

Explanation: In migrating to a cloud service architecture, your organization will want to review its existing Business Impact Analysis (BIA) and consider a new BIA, or at least a partial assessment, for cloud-specific concerns and the new risks and opportunities offered by the cloud. Some of the potential impacts are things you should have already included in your original BIA, but these may be more significant and take new forms in the cloud.

State notification laws and the loss of proprietary data/intellectual property pre-existed the cloud; only the lack of ability to transfer liability is new.

126. A

Explanation: IaaS entails the cloud customer installing and maintaining the OS, programs, and data.

127. A

Explanation: The BIA has to consider these risks for any operations migrated to the cloud. A large number of data for this part of the report have to be readily available and will not have to be re-created for the BIA, as it should have been performed as part of the **cost-benefit analysis** when the organization first considered migration.

128. A, C, and D

Explanation: All these options are affected by the terms of the cloud contract except for malware.

129. A, C, and D

Explanation: Many of the risks that exist in the public cloud are personnel threats (inadvertent and malicious), external threats, natural disasters, and so forth.

130. A, C, and D

Explanation: The following countermeasures for protecting cloud operations against internal threats are aggressive background checks, resume or reference confirmation, and skills and knowledge testing have to be conducted. For current employees, personnel policies have to be used that is comprehensive and recurring training.

131. A, B, and D

Explanation: The following countermeasures for protecting cloud operations against internal threats are:

- Active surveillance and monitoring programs, both physical and electronic, can be used
- Data has to be masked and obfuscated for all personnel who do not need to work directly with raw data

132. A, B, and D

Explanation: The following countermeasures for protecting cloud operations against internal threats are:

- For current employees, personnel policies have to be used that include comprehensive and recurring training, mandatory vacation and job rotation, and two-person integrity in those situations where it makes financial and operational sense.

- Stable workflow policies have to include separation of duties and least privilege

133. B, C, and D
Explanation: Most of the benefits of migrating to a public cloud configuration are the security offered by **fast replication, regular backups, and distributed, remote processing and storage of data** offered by cloud providers.

134. A, B, and D
Explanation: Extensive access control and authentication techniques and tools have to be implemented. Countermeasures also include analysis and review of all log data by trained, skilled personnel frequently, combined with automated tools such as SIEM, SIM, and SEM solutions.

135. B
Explanation: Attackers prefer Type 2 hypervisors because of the more significant surface area. They can attack the hypervisor itself, the underlying OS, and the machine directly.

136. B
Explanation: Vendor lock-out occurs when a cloud-customer is unable to recover or access his or her own data because of the cloud provider going into bankruptcy or otherwise leaving the market.

137. C
Explanation: Software developers typically install backdoors because of avoiding to perform the entire workflow when modifying the program they are currently working on; they typically leave backdoors behind in production software, inadvertently or intentionally.

138. A
Explanation: Logical design for data separation must be incorporated at the following levels:
- Compute Nodes
- Control Plane
- Management plane
- Network
- Storage Nodes

139. D
Explanation: The Uptime Institute Data Center Site Infrastructure Tier Standard Topology describes the name four-tiered architecture for data center design that is:
- **Tier I**: Basic Data Center Site Infrastructure
- **Tier II**: Redundant Site Infrastructure Capacity Components
- **Tier III**: Concurrently Maintainable Site Infrastructure
- **Tier IV**: Fault-Tolerant Site Infrastructure

140. B

Explanation: The American Society of Heating, Refrigeration, and Air Conditioning Engineers (ASHRAE) recommended range for temperature and humidity in a data center is:

- Low-end temperature 64.4° F (18° C)
- High-end temperature 80.6° F (27° C)
- Low-end moisture 40% relative humidity and 41.9° F (5.5° C) dew point
- High-end moisture 60% relative humidity and 59° F (15° C) dew point

141. A and C

Explanation: Numerous authentication methods are supported by iSCSI:

- Kerberos
- Secure Remote Password (SRP)
- The Simple Public-Key Mechanism (SPKM1/2)
- Challenge-Handshake Authentication Protocol (CHAP)

142. C

Explanation: The deployment and use of IPSec have main vital challenges that are:

- **Configuration Management**: The use of IPSec is optional. As such, most of the endpoint devices connecting to the cloud infrastructure do not have IPSec support enabled and configured. If IPSec is not enabled on the endpoint, then depending on the configuration choices made on the server side of the IPSec solution, the endpoint may not be able to connect and complete a transaction if it does not support IPSec. CSPs may not have the proper visibility on the customer endpoints or the server infrastructure to understand IPSec configurations. As a result, the ability to ensure the use of IPSec to secure network traffic may be limited
- **Performance**: The use of IPSec imposes a performance penalty on the systems deploying the technology. Although the impact on the performance of an average system is small, it is the cumulative effect of IPSec across an enterprise architecture, end to end, that must be evaluated before implementation

143. D

Explanation: Within a host cluster, resources are allocated and managed as if they were pooled or jointly available to all members of the cluster. The use of resource-sharing concepts such as **reservations, limits, and shares** may be used to further refine and orchestrate the allocation of resources according to requirements that the cluster administrator imposes. While **shares** provision the remaining resources left in a cluster when there is **resource contention**, specifically, shares allow the cluster's reservations to be allocated and then to address any remaining resources that may be available for use by members of the cluster through a prioritized percentage-based allocation mechanism.

144. A

Explanation: Maintenance mode is utilized when updating or configuring different components of the cloud environment. While in maintenance mode, customer access is blocked, and alerts are disabled, but logging is still enabled.

145. C
Explanation: NIST recommends three service models, which define the different foundational categories of cloud services:

- IaaS (Infrastructure as a Service)
- PaaS (Platform as a Service)
- SaaS (Software as a Service)

146. B
Explanation: A honeypot is used to detect, deflect, or in a similar manner counteract attempts at unauthorized use of information systems. In general, a honeypot consists of a computer, data, or a network site that appears to be part of a network but is isolated and monitored, and which seems to hold information or a resource of value to attackers.

147. A
Explanation: During a vulnerability assessment, the cloud environment is tested for known vulnerabilities. Detected vulnerabilities are not exploited during a vulnerability assessment (nondestructive testing) and may require further validation to detect false positives.

148. D
Explanation: The purpose of physical design is that it communicates decisions regarding hardware used to deliver a system. The following is right about a physical network design:

- It is created from a logical network design
- It often expands elements found in a logical design

149. B
Explanation: Configuration management needs to be tied to change management because change management has to approve modifications to all production systems before them taking place. Besides, there should never be a change that is allowed to take place to a Configuration Item (CI) in a production system unless change management has approved the change first.

150. A and B
Explanation: Change management has numerous objectives:

- Respond to a customer's changing business requirements while maximizing value and reducing incidents, disruption, and rework
- Respond to business, and IT requests for change that aligns services with business needs
- Ensure that changes are recorded and evaluated
- Ensure that authorized changes are prioritized, planned, tested, implemented, documented, and reviewed in a controlled manner
- Ensure that all changes to CIs are recorded in the configuration management system

- Optimize overall business risk. It is often correct to minimize business risk, but sometimes it is appropriate to knowingly accept risk because of the potential benefit

151. A

Explanation: According to the ITIL framework: **"An incident is defined as an unplanned interruption to an IT service or a reduction in the quality of an IT service"**.

152. D

Explanation: BC is the capability of the organization to continue delivery of products or services at acceptable predefined levels following a disruptive incident while BCM is a holistic management process that identifies potential threats to an organization and the impacts to business operations those threats, if realized, might cause. It provides a framework for building organizational resilience with the capability of an effective response that safeguards the interests of its key stakeholders, reputation, brand, and value-creating activities.

153. B

Explanation: The risk-management process has four components:

- Framing risk
- Assessing risk
- Responding to risk
- Monitoring risk

154. C

Explanation: An organization will conduct a risk assessment (or risk analysis) to evaluate the followings:

- Threats to its assets
- Vulnerabilities present in the environment
- The likelihood that a threat will be realized by taking advantage of exposure (or probability and frequency when dealing with quantitative assessment)
- The impact that the exposure being realized will have on the organization
- Countermeasures available that can minimize the threat's ability to exploit the exposure or that can lessen the impact to the organization when a threat can exploit a vulnerability
- The residual risk, or the amount of risk that is left over when appropriate controls are appropriately applied to lessen or remove the vulnerability

155. D

Explanation: Due diligence is the act of investigating and understanding the risks the company faces. For instance, a company practices due care by developing security policies, procedures, and standards. Due care shows that a company has taken responsibility for the activities that take place within the corporation and has taken the necessary steps to help protect the company, its resources, and employees from possible risks.

Therefore, due diligence is understanding the existing threats and risks, and due care is implementing countermeasures to protect from those threats. If a company does not practice due care and due

diligence about the security of its assets, it can be legally charged with negligence and held accountable for any ramifications of that negligence.

156. B
Explanation: A vulnerability is a lack of a countermeasure or a weakness in a countermeasure that is in place. A threat is any potential danger that is associated with the exploitation of a vulnerability. The threat is that someone, or something, will identify a specific vulnerability and use it against the company or individual. A risk is the likelihood of a threat agent exploiting a vulnerability and the corresponding business impact.

157. C
Explanation: A formula of calculating for SLE is:

SLE = asset value (in $) × exposure factor (loss due to successful threat exploit, as a %)

158. C
Explanation: Once an incident is identified, the process of performing digital forensics is:

- Collection
- Examination
- Analysis
- Reporting

159. A
Explanation: The cloud provider only owns the hardware and supplies the utilities in the IaaS service model, and the customer is responsible for the OS, programs, and data.

160. A, B, and C
Explanation: The cloud service provider might share all of these options except security control administration.

161. A
Explanation: The contract among the provider and customer maximize the customer's trust by holding the provider financially liable for negligence or insufficient service while the customer remains legally liable for all inadvertent disclosures.

162. D
Explanation: Cloud customers are more likely to see a SOC 3 report because it contains no actual data about the security controls of the audit target and is instead just an assertion that the audit was conducted and that the target organization was passed.

163. B

Explanation: SOC 2 Type 2 is the sort of report that is extremely useful for getting a valid assessment of an organization's security posture. This report is much more detailed and will most likely be kept closely held by the provider.

164. C
Explanation: SOX was the Congressional response to some high-profile perfidy in several corporate cases, including WorldCom and Adelphia, that transpired in the late 1990's and early 2000's.

165. A, B, and D
Explanation: Hardening the operating system means making it more secure. Limiting administrator access, closing unused ports, and removing unnecessary services and libraries all have the potential to make an OS more secure.

166. A, B, and D
Explanation: All these options enhanced the cloud customer(s) trust to the cloud provider.

167. A, B, and C
Explanation: User access to the cloud environment can be administrated to the following ways or can be implemented to some methods that can be enabled to the user access:
- Customer directly administers access
- Provider provides administration on behalf of the customer
- The third party provides administration on behalf of the customer

168. B
Explanation: SOC 2 reports are specifically intended to report audits of any controls on an organization's security, availability, processing integrity, confidentiality, and privacy. Therefore, a cloud provider intending to prove its trustworthiness would look to a SOC 2 report as the artifact that demonstrated it.

169. C
Explanation: SOC 3 contains no actual data about the security controls of the audit target and is instead just an assertion that the audit was conducted and that the target organization passed.

170. C
Explanation: The provider can enable the customer to access audit and performance logs or to even configure settings of these, on resources limited to that customer's use.

171. A
Explanation: The customer always owns the data and will therefore always have access to it.

172. D
Explanation: Security is always dependent on business drivers and beholden to operational needs.

173. B
Explanation: A customer is responsible for protecting that information and is ultimately liable for any unauthorized disclosure of that data.

174. A
Explanation: Good understanding of the physical layout and site controls could be of excellent use to an attacker. Consequently they are kept extremely confidential.

175. B
Explanation: Open source software is available to the public, and typically draws inspection from many, disparate reviewers.

176. A, B, and C
Explanation: Firewalls can use rules, behavior analytics, and content filtering techniques to determine which traffic is allowable.

177. C
Explanation: Honeypots is usually a dummy machine with useless data, partially secured and configured as if it was a realistic portion of the production environment.

178. C
Explanation: Vulnerability assessments cannot prevent attackers from discovering unknown vulnerabilities in systems and attacking them. These type of attacks are typically referred to as zero-day exploits.

179. A
Explanation: The EU Directive 95/46/EC provides for the regulation of the protection and free Movement of personal data within the European Union. This directive applies to data processed by automated, which means and data contained in paper files. It does not apply to the processing of data in these instances:

- By a natural person in the course of purely personal or household activities
- In the course of an activity that falls outside the scope of community law, such as operations concerning public safety, defense, or state security

180. B and D
Explanation: From a contractual, regulated, and PII perspective, the followings have to be reviewed and entirely understood by the CCSP about any hosting contracts (as well as the other overarching components within an SLA):

- Scope of processing
- Use of subcontractors
- Deletion of data

- Proper or required data security control
- Locations of data
- Return or restitution of data
- Right to audit subcontractors

181. B

Explanation: An audit scope statement delivers the required level of information for the cloud service customer or organization subject to the audit to completely understand (and agree with) the scope, focus, and type of assessment being performed. Typically, an audit scope statement includes the followings:

- General statement of focus and objectives
- The scope of audit (including exclusions)
- Type of audit (certification, attestation, etc.)
- Security assessment requirements
- Assessment criteria (including ratings)
- Acceptance criteria
- Deliverables
- Classification (confidential, highly confidential, secret, top secret, public, etc.)

The audit scope statement can also catalog the circulation list, as well as key individuals associated with the audit.

182. C

Explanation: Many stages are performed before commencing a gap analysis review. Although they can vary reliant on the review, common stages include the followings:

- Obtain management support from the right managers
- Define the scope and objectives
- Plan an assessment schedule
- Agree on a plan
- Conduct information gathering exercises
- Interview key personnel
- Review supporting documentation
- Verify the information obtained
- Identify any potential risks
- Document the findings
- Develop a report and recommendations
- Present the report
- Sign off and accept the report

183. D

Explanation: ISO/IEC 27018 deals with the privacy aspects of consumer cloud computing. ISO 27018 is the first international set of cloud-based privacy controls. As a new component of the ISO 27001 standard, ISO 27018 was published on 30 July 2014.

Cloud security professionals adopting ISO/IEC 27018 have to be aware of the following five fundamental principles:

- Consent
- Control
- Transparency
- Communication
- Independent and yearly audit

184. D

Explanation: The following domains are ISO 27001:2013, the world's most widely used ISMS implementation standard:

- A.5—Security Policy Management
- A.6—Corporate Security Management
- A.7—Personnel Security Management
- A.8—Organizational Asset Management
- A.9—Information Access Management
- A.10—Cryptography Policy Management
- A.11—Physical Security Management
- A.12—Operational Security Management
- A.13—Network Security Management
- A.14—System Security Management
- A.15—Supplier Relationship Management
- A.16—Security Incident Management
- A.17—Security Continuity Management
- A.18—Security Compliance Management

185. A

Explanation: The following are vital data management roles:

- **Data Subject**: This is an individual who is the address of personal data
- **Data Controller**: This is an individual who either alone or jointly with other persons determines the purposes for which and how any personal data is processed
- **Data Processor**: About personal data, this is any person other than a data controller employee who processes the data on the data controller's behalf
- **Data Stewards**: These people are commonly responsible for data content, context, and associated business rules
- **Data Custodians**: These people are responsible for the safe custody, transport, data storage, and implementation of business rules.
- **Data Owners**: These people hold legal rights and complete control over a single piece or set of data elements. Data owners can also define distribution and associated policies.

186. C

Explanation: The following content and topics should be covered as a minimum within an SLA:

- Availability
- Performance
- Security and privacy of the data
- Logging and reporting
- Disaster recovery expectations
- Location of the data
- Data format and structure
- Portability of the data
- Identification and problem resolution
- Change-management process
- Dispute-mediation process
- Exit strategy with expectations

187. B
Explanation: The characteristics of the REST model include the following:

- It is lightweight
- It uses simple URLs
- It is not reliant on XML
- It is scalable
- It outputs in many formats (CSV, JSON, and so on)
- It is efficient, which means it uses smaller messages than XML

188. A, C, and D
Explanation: SDLC has the following core stages that are:

- Defining
- Designing
- Development
- Testing

189. A, B, and C
Explanation: The STRIDE threat model has the following components that are:

- Spoofing
- Tampering
- Repudiation
- Information disclosure
- Denial of service
- Elevation of privilege

190. C
Explanation: Static Application Security Testing (SAST) is a useful method of security application testing. Static means that all source code, byte code, and binaries are tested without the application being executed. For known security flaws and vulnerabilities, these code sources are examined to try to

catch them before going into production. This type of testing is often used in the early stages of application development as there is no other way to test the full application at that time.

191. B
Explanation: All these answers are correct, but B is the best answer, because it is the most general answer, includes the other answers, and is, therefore, the best choice. This is an excellent example of the question type that may appear on the actual exam.

192. C
Explanation: Sandboxing refers to the concept of a protected area used to test untested or untrusted code or to understand better whether the application works as intended.

193. B
Explanation: Identity management is the process by which individuals have access to system resources through the associating of user rights with a given identity.

194. A
Explanation: The identity provider is the trusted third party in the federation's trusted third party model, and each member organization within the federation are the relying parties.

195. B
Explanation: The Organizational Normative Framework (ONF) is a container framework for all components of security of an application, best practices, cataloged and leveraged by the organization.

196. C
Explanation: An Application Program Interface (API) is a set of routines, protocols, and tools for building software applications.

197. B
Explanation: Together with the ONF, the application normative framework (ANF) is used to create it for a specific application. The ANF shares the relevant parts of the ONF needed to achieve the required level of security and level of trust required by an application.
The relationship between ANF and ONF is one-to-one; each application has an ANF mapping back to the ONF. The relationship between ONF and ANF, however, is one-to-many. The ONF has many ANFs, but only one ONF is available to the ANF.

198. B
Explanation: Security Assertion Markup Language (SAML) is an XML-based framework for communicating information about authentication, authorization or entitlement and assigning information across organizations.

199. B

Explanation: ISO / IEC 27034 - 1, "Information Technology – Security Techniques – Application Security," is one of the most widely accepted set of standards and guidelines for secure development of applications.

200. C

Explanation: Data masking is a method of creating a structurally similar but inauthentic version of data from an organization that can be used for purposes such as software testing and user training.

201. A

Explanation: DAMs can either be agent-based or network-based, meaning an agent resides on the database machine or instance, or a network agent monitors traffic from and to the database.

202. C

Explanation: WAFs detect how the application interacts with the environment, making it ideal for detecting and refuting things such as SQL injection and XSS.

203. D

Explanation:

- Multifactor authentication consists of at least two of the following aspects — something you know, something you are, or something you have. Something you know can be a password, a passphrase, etc.
- Something you have can like a number - generating key fob, a smartphone capable of receiving text messages, or even a telephone capable of receiving a call and then transmitting a number or key to the individual, but accessible only from a particular telephone number
- Something you are as a living creature is a biometric trait of yourself. This may be as unique and specific as the fingerprint of your DNA or as general as a photograph

204. C

Explanation: SOAP is a protocol specification providing for the exchange of structured information or data in web services. It also works over other protocols such as SMTP, FTP, and HTTP. Some of the characteristics of SOAP include the followings:

- Standards-based
- Reliant on XML
- Highly intolerant of errors
- Slower
- Built-in error handling

205. B

Explanation: As the code is not revealed, DAST is considered a black-box test and the test must look for problems and vulnerabilities while the application is running. It is most effective when used against standard HTTP and other HTML web application interfaces.

206. A

Explanation: Sandboxing refers to the concept of a protected area used to test untested or untrusted code or to understand better whether the application works as intended or not.

207. A

Explanation: There are four tiers of the Uptime Institute's data center redundancy rating system, while Tier 1 is a simplistic datacenter, with little or no redundancy and is labeled Basic Site Infrastructure. It is the lowest tier of data center redundancy.

208. C

Explanation: A power generator for extended electrical outages, with at least 12 hours of fuel to run the generator at sufficient load to power the IT systems.

209. B, C, and D

Explanation: The most common types of security trainings are initial, recurring, and refresher.

210. A

Explanation:

STRIDE threat model has the following parts:

- Spoofing
- Tampering
- Repudiation
- Information disclosure
- DoS
- Elevation of privilege

211. C

Explanation: STRIDE threat model has the following parts:

- Spoofing
- Tampering
- Repudiation
- Information disclosure
- DoS
- Elevation of privilege

212. B

Explanation: SAST has nothing to do with team building; all the rest of the answers are SAST features.

213. D

Explanation: DAST has nothing to do with binary inspection; all the rest of the answers are DAST features.

214. A

Explanation: Keystroke logging is not a feature of secure KVM design; in fact, secure KVM components should mitigate keystroke logging potential. All the rest of the answers are secure KVM components characteristics.

215. C

Explanation: Redundancy in emergency egress is the only feature in data centers of any type that may be found; all other features of the answer list may be found in certain levels only.

216. B

Explanation: Regardless of the tier level or purpose of any data center, design focus for security have always to consider health and human safety paramount.

217. B

Explanation: In most RAID configurations, all data is stored across the various disks in a method known as striping. In some RAID schemes, parity bits are added to the raw data to aid in recovery after a drive failure.

218. A

Explanation: Cross training provides a reduction in the capacity of lost contingency by ensuring that employees can perform critical tasks even if they are not assigned mainly in full times.

219. C

Explanation: Changing regulations do not have the outcome in lack of availability.

220. C

Explanation: Documentation on the security training can be used to show that staff has received adequate, pertinent training to a suitable level, which demonstrates due diligence—that is, effort in furtherance of due care.

221. D

Explanation: The location of various datacenters (rurally situated, distant from metropolitan areas) may create challenges for searching multiple power utility providers and ISPs, as those areas that are not usually served by multiple vendors.

222. D

Explanation: Some of the physical security aspects that ought to be included in the design include the following:

- Vehicular approach/access
- Guest/visitor access through a controlled entry point
- Proper placement of hazardous or vital resources

- Interior physical access controls
- Specific physical protections for highly sensitive assets
- Fire detection and suppression systems
- Sufficient power for all these functions

223. B
Explanation: Chinese wall model is also known as the Brewer-Nash security model.

224. B
Explanation: Type 2 is a software hypervisor, and it runs on top of the OS that runs on a host device. Attackers prefer Type 2 hypervisors because of the larger surface area. They can attack the hypervisor itself, the underlying OS, and the machine directly.

225. C
Explanation: Data dispersion is a technique, where data is divided into "chunks" that are encrypted as well as the parity bits and then written to various drives in the cloud cluster.

226. C
Explanation: All organizations take part in an unscheduled, unannounced practice scenario, performing their full BC/DR activities. This is known as a Full Test.

227. A
Explanation: The essential participants work together at a scheduled time to describe how they would perform their tasks in a given BC/DR scenario. It has the least impact on the production of the testing alternatives.

228. C
Explanation: Liquid propane does not spoil, which obviates the necessity for constantly refreshing and restocking it and might make it more cost-effective.

229. B
Explanation: A data center with less than optimum humidity can have a higher static electricity discharge rate.

230. D
Explanation: UPS should last long enough for graceful shutdown of affected systems.

231. C
Explanation: Generator power has to be online before battery backups fail. The specific amount of time will vary between datacenters.

232. B

Explanation: Speed is the automatic patching characteristic because of automated patching is much faster and more efficient than manual patching. However, it is not necessarily any less expensive than manual patching.

233. C
Explanation: Checklists serve numerous purposes. They describe the specific actions necessary, they can be aligned in order of execution, and they can create a record, after the activity is complete, of actions taken, by whom, and when (if each checklist step is annotated with the time and initials of the person completing the action as it occurs).

234. B, C, and D
Explanation: The CMB has to be composed of representatives from all stakeholders within the organization. Recommended representatives include personnel from IT, security, legal, management, the user group, finance and acquisition, and HR.

235. A, B, and C
Explanation: Most operating systems have basic toolsets for monitoring performance and events. These can include CPU usage, memory usage, disk space, and disk I/O timing.

236. A, C, and D
Explanation: When a system or device is put into maintenance mode, the data center operator must ensure the following tasks are successful:

- All operational instances are removed
- Prevent all new logins
- Ensure logging is continued

237. B
Explanation: UPS offer a line conditioning capability because of line conditioning is a function of UPS, and it often serves as an additional component of normal operations, dampening surges and dips in utility power automatically.

238. A
Explanation: The entire deviations from the baseline have to be documented, including details of the investigation and outcome.

239. A
Explanation: The more systems are included in the baseline, the more cost-effective and scalable the baseline is.

240. C

Explanation: Joint operating agreements can be used to establish cost-effective relocation sites at facilities belonging to other operations in the local area if the event or disaster only affects your organization's campus.

241. D
Explanation: 12 hours is a minimum time to take a generator fuel storage for a cloud datacenter dictates by the Uptime Institute.

242. A, B, and D
Explanation: A BC/DR kit should contain the followings:
- A current copy of the plan
- A small number of emergency essentials (flashlight, water, rations, and so on)
- Copies of all appropriate network and infrastructure diagrams and architecture
- Copies of all requisite software for creating a clean build of the critical systems
- Documentation tools and equipment
- Emergency and backup communication equipment.
- Emergency contact information
- Fresh batteries are sufficient for operating all powered equipment in the kit for at least 24 hours

243. D
Explanation: Conducting forensic analysis in a cloud environment is the least challenge as it refers to the analysis of data once it is obtained.

244. A
Explanation: Controls that are designed to comply with laws and regulations whether they be local or international, are called the legal controls.

245. D
Explanation: Plausibility is a distractor and not specifically relevant to cloud forensics.

246. D
Explanation: There is nothing to do with the value of the data itself, even if they may have a value associated with it, as part of contract PII.

247. B
Explanation: The best example of regulated PII component is mandatory breach reporting.

248. D
Explanation: Quality is not associated with security. Others are.

249. A

Explanation: Independence is the superior benefit of external audit. External audits are often more independent and therefore lead to more effective results.

250. C
Explanation: SOX was passed primarily to address the issues of fraudulent accounting practices, poor audit practices, inadequate financial controls, and poor oversight by governing boards of directors.

251. A
Explanation: Before SOX, the AICPA audit standard for reviewing publicly traded corporations was called the SAS 70. SOX mandated a high number of new components for audits, so the AICPA created a new standard that superseded the SAS 70, and that standard is SSAE 16.

252. A
Explanation: SOC 1 reports are a focus on auditing the financial reporting instruments of a corporation.

253. D
Explanation: The SOC 3 is the seal of approval. It contains no actual data concerning the security controls of the audit target and is instead just an assertion that the audit was conducted and that the target organization passed.

254. A
Explanation: The objective of gap analysis is to start the benchmarking process against risk and security standards and frameworks.

255. D
Explanation: Generally Accepted Accounting Practices (GAAP) are created and maintained by the AICPA, which auditors and accountants adhere to in their professions.

256. A
Explanation: GLBA provides a superior provision for specifying the many types of protection and controls that financial institutions are necessary to use for securing customers' account information.

257. C
Explanation: Highly regulated industries such as banking, law enforcement, high-level government agencies, etc. Therefore, wholesale and distribution is not the example of a highly regulated environment.

258. B
Explanation: A SOC Type I report address a specific point in time as opposed to a report of effectiveness over a period.

259. D
Explanation: A SOC Type II report addresses a specific period as opposed to a specific point in time.

260. A

Explanation: The right to be forgotten principle specify any individual can notify any entity that has PII for that individual and instruct that entity to delete and destroy all of that individual's PII in that entity's control.

261. A

Explanation: The right to audit has to be contained in the client Service-Level Agreement (SLA).

262. D

Explanation: SOX was enacted fraudulent accounting practices, poor audit practices, inadequate financial controls, and poor oversight by governing boards of directors.

263. C

Explanation: The essential component of GLBA was the creation of a formal information security program.

264. D

Explanation: HIPPA are not specified financial controls.

265. A

Explanation: The Doctrine of the Proper Law is a term used to describe the processes associated with determining what legal jurisdiction will hear a dispute when one occurs.

266. A

Explanation: The Restatement (Second) Conflict of Law is a collation of developments in common law that assist the courts to stay up with changes. Numerous states have conflicting laws, and judges use these restatements to help them in determining which laws have to be applied when conflicts occur.

267. D

Explanation: The Stored Communication Act passed in 1995, is an older law, in bad need of updating, and unclear about newer technologies.

268. B

Explanation: The lowest level is Level 1, which is self-assessment.

269. B

Explanation: Key Risk Indicators (KRI) are those items that will be the first things that let you know something is amiss. It might be the announcement of the discovery of a new vulnerability that could affect your cloud provider. The purpose is that you must identify and closely monitor the things that will most quickly alert you to a change in the risk environment.

270. A

Explanation: ISO 31000:2009 is an international standard that focuses on designing, implementing, and reviewing the risk management processes and practices.

271. C

Explanation: ENISA identify the top eight security risks based on likelihood and impact:

- Loss of governance
- Lock-in
- Isolation failure
- Compliance risk
- Management interface failure
- Data protection
- Malicious insider
- Insecure or incomplete data deletion

272. A, C, and D

Explanation: The CSA STAR program also consists of three levels based on the Open Certification Framework:

- Self-assessment
- Third-party assessment-based certification
- Continuous monitoring–based certification

273. B

Explanation: ISO 28000:2007 defines a set of security management requirements, including those that need to be applied to all parties within a supply chain.

274. A, and B

Explanation: There are many risk management frameworks exist that are designed to help the organization in developing sound risk management practices and management. Some of the common risk management frameworks are:

- NIST 800-37
- European Union Agency for Network and Information Security (ENISA)

275. D

Explanation: A threat coupled with a vulnerability is the best definition of a risk.

276. D

Explanation: ENISA identify the top eight security risks based on likelihood and impact:

- Loss of governance
- Lock-in
- Isolation failure
- Compliance risk

- Management interface failure
- Data protection
- Malicious insider
- Insecure or incomplete data deletion

277. D

Explanation: Avoidance is not a method for handling risk; it means leaving a business opportunity because the risk is simply too high and cannot be compensated for with sufficient control mechanisms.

278. B

Explanation: Cloud carriers are the intermediary who provides connectivity and transport of the ISPs between the cloud customer and the cloud provider.

279. A

Explanation: Transference is associated with insurance because of the following reason:
The organization pays someone else to accept the risk, at a lower cost than the potential impact that would result from the risk being realized; this is usually in the form of insurance.

280. C

Explanation: The use of subcontractors can add risk to the supply chain and have to be considered; trusting the provider's management of their vendors and suppliers (including subcontractors) is significant to trusting the provider.

281. A

Explanation: The data custodian is any organization or individual who manipulates, stores, or moves the data for the data owner. Within the organization, a data custodian might be a database administrator.

282. A

Explanation: Organizations have four main ways to address risk:

- Mitigating
- Accepting
- Transferring
- Avoidance

283. A

Explanation: Hex is a fictional computer featured in the Discworld novels by Terry Pratchett. So, it is not a part of the risk management framework.

284. B

Explanation: Roles and responsibilities have to be included in the contract, not the SLA. Therefore, it is a superior method to determine whether something might belong in the SLA at all is figuring out

whether a numerical value is associated with it. In this case, the component includes names and offices (roles), not numerical values, so it is immediately recognizable as something that is not appropriate for the SLA.

285. A
Explanation: The CSA CCM is an inventory of cloud service security controls that are arranged into separate security domains.

286. A
Explanation: The organization can consider and use different types of controls when choosing to mitigate risk. In the security perspective, we usually group controls into three general types:

- Physical
- Technical
- Administrative

Therefore, Transitional is not types of controls.

287. A
Explanation: An IT analyst is generally not high enough of a position that can provide quality information to other stakeholders.

About Our Products

Other Network & Security related products from IPSpecialist LTD are:

- CCNA Routing & Switching Technology Workbook
- CCNA Security Technology Workbook
- CCNA Service Provider Technology Workbook
- CCDA Technology Workbook
- CCDP Technology Workbook
- CCNP Route Technology Workbook
- CCNP Switch Technology Workbook
- CCNP Troubleshoot Technology Workbook
- CCNP Security SENSS Technology Workbook
- CCNP Security SIMOS Technology Workbook
- CCNP Security SITCS Technology Workbook
- CCNP Security SISAS Technology Workbook
- CompTIA Network+ Technology Workbook
- CompTIA Security+ Technology Workbook
- EC-Council CEH v10 2nd Edition Technology Workbook
- CCNA CyberOps SECFND Technology Workbook
- Certified Block Chain Expert Technology Workbook

Upcoming products are:

- CCNA CyberOps SECOPS Technology Workbook
- Certified Application Security Engineer (Java) Technology Workbook
- CompTIA Pentest+ Technology Workbook
- CompTIA Cloud Essentials Technology Workbook
- CompTIA Cloud+ Technology Workbook

Note from the Author:

Reviews are gold to authors! If you have enjoyed this book and it has helped you along certification, would you consider rating and reviewing it?

Link to Product Page:

www.ingramcontent.com/pod-product-compliance
Lightning Source LLC
Chambersburg PA
CBHW080429060326
40689CB00019B/4433